HAND TO MOU

THE TRADITIONAL FOOD OF THE SCOTTISH ISLANDS

HAND TO MOUTH

THE TRADITIONAL FOOD OF THE SCOTTISH ISLANDS

JANE CHEAPE

First published in Scotland in 2002
by Acair Ltd, 7 James Street,
Stornoway, Scotland. HS1 2QN

Tel: 01851 70 3020
Fax: 01851 70 3294
E-mail: acair@virginbiz.com
www.acairbooks.com

A CIP catalogue record for this title is available from the British Library.

ISBN: 0 86152 727 5

Cover and book design Margaret Anne MacLeod, Acair Ltd.

Printed by ColourBooks Ltd., Dublin

CONTENTS

	Preface	7
	Acknowledgements	9
	Introduction	10
Chapter 1	Staffs of Life	13
Chapter 2	Pots, Pans and Fireplaces	28
Chapter 3	Potatoes: Starch and Sedition	44
Chapter 4	Dairying	55
Chapter 5	Fish	68
Chapter 6	Meat	82
Chapter 7	Wildfowling	95
Chapter 8	Conclusions: " ... famine in their aspect ... "	110
	Bibliography	129
	Index	134

For
Annie,
Jessie
&
Ronald

Preface

Twenty-four years ago I made my first visit to the Outer Hebrides. It was the Glasgow Fair fortnight. We sailed at noon on the Oban to Lochboisdale ferry into an unfriendly sea and freshening wind. By the time the *Columba* was leaving Castlebay darkness had set in. We walked the rain-soaked deck to keep away sea-sickness. It was after ten o'clock before thin arms of land were faintly visible and another hour before we reached our destination, Kilbride, South Uist.

It was an inauspicious beginning to a wonderful visit. For the next fortnight the sun split the wide Hebridean sky and we explored the south end of the island on foot. From Lùdag, we took the ferry to Barra and Eriskay. At night, drunk with light and air, we ate the food of the country and fell into bed.

There were three black cows on the croft, hand-milked twice daily. Hens invaded the kitchen. Out on the machair, where the soil is light, vegetables grew. On the beach, a stone's throw from the house, children collected winkles for the van which came weekly to take shellfish to southern markets and pay the pickers pocket money. Sheep slaughtered quietly behind the byre were slow-cooked in the peat-fired Rayburn. The flavour of that mutton was unforgettable. A bucket of herring arrived from a passing fisherman. Quickly gutted by expert hands the fish were hung on a string in the wind to dry off before being coated in oatmeal and put in the frying pan.

North of Kilbride, at a place called Drimore, archeologists have excavated a mound known as *A' Cheàrdach Mhòr*, the Big Smiddy. Here the earliest pastoralists have left their mark; from pots and querns to the contents of their rubbish heaps. The remnants of their meals are unfailingly familiar. There are fishbones - but not many. Fishing was dangerous, as it still is. Shellfish debris in profusion, scallop, oyster, razor, winkle and whelk show how these early settlers maximised the harvest of the rocks. It is easy to think of them combing the pools, one eye always looking out to sea for danger. Red deer and their antlers abounded. Sheep remains, akin to the Soay and Shetland type, were common. Tenuous evidence suggests that the cattle grazing around the wheelhouse were similar to the old Highland Black Cattle, or Kyloes. Gannet, shag and puffin had all been in the pot - a food source that survived well into this century - supporting those living literally closest to the edge; by the cliffs of St. Kilda or Mingulay.

I make no apology, therefore, for the use of the word traditional in this title. The food of the Hebrides and the Northern Isles is as old as the islands' settlements. Wherever we live now, we are besieged by the culture of the supermarket, and nowhere more so than in those areas where transport is expensive, outlets fewer and choice restricted. But bere bannocks and home-made cheese can still be found in Orkney. There is plenty of venison in Skye and prawns are fished between the islands of Eigg and Canna. There is a black pig in Muck, which has just farrowed. There is still carrageen, and the wild brambles in Bute are magnificent.

This book aims to examine the food which sustained a people in a harsh and remote landscape. Sea, cliffs, beach, hill, byre, coop and lazy-bed, each had its own harvest.

And finally, we can no longer ignore that gastronomic latecomer, that loose cannon, the potato. These unfamiliar tubers did not arrive in the Hebrides until about 1750. Initially, they were not well received. Later, they were to play a disproportionate role in Highland and especially Hebridean history. When they failed, the Islands became the epicentre of famine. Today the silverweed (Potentilla Anserina) that spreads its grey-green foliage over Hebridean beaches is a reminder of the people who roasted its roots and ate them, to quell their pangs of hunger.

Acknowledgements

I owe a debt of gratitude to Mrs Mary Kate Morrison of West Kilbride, South Uist, Miss Joy Sandison of Unst, Professor Alexander Fenton of the European Ethnological Research Centre in the National Museums of Scotland and to Hugh Cheape.

Introduction

'In their food, clothing, and in the whole of their domestic economy, they adhere to ancient parsimony.' (1549)

Monro's Western Isles of Scotland, ed. R.W. Monro, Edinburgh 1961 p.42

Most of the Highlands and Islands of Scotland are composed of hard, primary rocks. The Lewisian gneiss, being some of the oldest rocks in the world, make up the larger part of the Outer Hebrides. They provide an impermeable and acidic layer, now covered by a recent, deep overlay of peat. Even those areas which geologically may appear more favoured, such as the tertiary basalts, are so weathered and exposed as to make cultivation difficult.

The Atlantic littoral has been described by many island observers since the sixteenth century. Some, like Boswell and Johnson or the cheery Richard Kearton were true travellers. Walter Scott was a romantic. Some were statisticians like Martin Martin, some protoscientists like Thomas Pennant, some impatient 'improvers' like Dr. John Walker. The eye of bureaucracy was cast over the communities by the Church in the Old and New Statistical Accounts and later by philanthropists and by government. Almost invariably they note the numbers of cattle and the potential of the sea. Any cropping they admire and seek to encourage. In truth the Hebrides were as much grazing country as the mainland Highlands and arable little more than a snatched opportunity.

From the neolithic period settlement hugged the coast where in addition to ready access to inshore fishing some areas possessed the much vaunted machair grasslands, a lime-rich loam mixed with shell sand, locally intensively dunged with seaweed manure. But even in these favoured areas exposure to the vagaries of climate made arable cultivation more difficult than any commentators would have us believe.

The Northern Isles are also on primary rock, mainly of a metamorphosed sandstone which gives this complex archipelago its gentle rolling appearance. In Orkney the soils are enriched by the effects of glacial drift.

This whole region lives in the path of the great sweep north of the Atlantic Drift, which brings warmth to air and sea. Until Dean Monro's account of 1549 it was an unknown country. The early Scottish historians spoke of these islands only from hearsay, knowing little of the geography that might illuminate the history. Yet perhaps nowhere in the British Isles does geography weigh so heavily on history and the land weigh so heavily on the people. The myth of 'the verie profitable isle' should perhaps be laid at Monro's feet. This book is about the food they worked so hard to win.

Winnowing grain, Shetland, c.1900.

Chapter 1: Staffs of Life

Their native bread is made of oats, or barley. Of oatmeal they spread very thin cakes, coarse and hard, to which unaccustomed palates are not easily reconciled. The barley cakes are thicker and softer; I began to eat them without unwillingness; the blackness of their colour raises some dislike, but the taste is not disagreeable.

Johnson and Boswell, *Journey to the Western Islands of Scotland,* Oxford 1930 p.49

Brochan (porridge) ... taken with some bread is the constant food of several thousands of both sexes in this (Skye) and other isles, during the winter and spring; yet they undergo many fatigues both by sea and land, and are very healthful.

Martin Martin, *A Description of the Western Islands of Scotland circa 1695*, Edinburgh 1994 p.242

... Above a thousand pounds worth of meal is annually imported, a famine threatened at this time; but was prevented by the seasonable arrival of a mealship; and the inhabitants like the sons of Jacob of old, flocked down to buy food.

Pennant Thomas, *A Tour in Scotland and Voyage to the Hebrides, 1772*, Edinburgh 1998 p.217

Round, flat, thickish cakes of either barleymeal, oatmeal, pease-meal or a combination of grains, mixed quickly with water or milk and cooked on a flat stone or girdle were the staple food of the Islands. Dean Munro describes them as,

> a kind of bread, not unpleasant to the taste of oats and barley, the only grain cultivated in these regions, and from long practice, they have attained a considerable skill in moulding the cakes. [1]

The 'cakes' he tasted are roundly known as bannocks. In Orkney they might be known as a *foal* and in Shetland as a *tivlach* - where bannock was not used for oatmeal cakes. The Gaelic, *bonnach*, *bannach*, is probably from the old Scots, bannok, a cake.[2] As the poet, Robert Burns declared, Scotland was a land of cakes. 'Scone' implies that either the mixture has been divided up before cooking or after. In Orkney the word indicates a pancake. To understand the role of bannocks as the solid staple, it is worth noting that all other cereal-based porridges, gruels or soups were known in the Northern Isles as *speun mate* (eaten with a spoon).[3]

Among the cave-dwellers of Wick Bay during the mid-nineteenth century Dr. Arthur Mitchell (1826-1909) Deputy Commissioner in Lunacy in Scotland saw the bannock in its simplest form in the making.

> One of the women was busy baking. She mixed the oatmeal and water in a tin dish, spread the cake out on a flat stone which served her for a table, and, placing the cake against another stone, toasted it at the open fire of turf and wood.[4]

Thomas Pennant (1726-1798) a century earlier noted how in the Small Isles,

> They knead their bannock with water only and bake or rather toast it, by laying it upright against a stone placed near the fire.[5]

The ancient tradition of mixing grain and water, assessing the heat of the fire and the length of cooking is the basis of all baking. Instinct plays its part in the feel and look of the mixture and in the speed of preparation.

'Noo, bairns, let's hae a steer-up', was the prelude to one of Jeannie's bakings. One small girl asked to be taught how to make scones – and the following is the never-to-be forgotten recipe she was given:

> "Tak some floor in a bowl." "How much?" "Weel, maybe a peerie corn mair. Yea, yon would be aboot richt. Noo tak a little Baking Soda." "How much?" "Weel, a peerie scaar, and a grain of Cream of tartar in your leuf. Stir it all together and add some sour milk." "How much sour milk?" "Weel, no ower muckle," was the illuminating reply.[6]

Before the seventeenth century, bere, being the four or six-rowed barley, was the commonest grain crop in the islands. It is a hardy crop, being disease resistant, and less easily weather-damaged than oats, particularly if thinly sown. From earliest times bere had a reputation for heavy cropping. Adomnan the saint's biographer, records how St. Columba, who had offended a lay neighbour of his on the island of Iona by taking wattle from his field without asking permission, sent him as recompense six measures of barley to sow. But the sowing season had passed. "How shall a crop sown after midsummer succeed, against the nature of the land?"[7] But the barley, although sown on the fifteenth of June was indeed ready for reaping at the beginning of August. This 'miracle' illustrates what barley could do in optimum conditions. The minister of Harris, in the Old Statistical Account (1791-1799) confirmed how

> Weak stubble ground, manured with sea-weed, which is cast ashore in May, is sometimes ploughed down so late as the 10th or 12th of June, and yields excellent barley.[8]

Martin Martin (c.1660-1719) who travelled the Western Isles at the end of the seventeenth century was continually impressed by the barley crops he encountered. On Berneray, in the Sound of Harris,

> I found the product of barley to be sometimes twentyfold and upwards, and at that time all the east side of the island produce thirty fold.[9]

The laird of Harris confirmed the opinion of the people. Sir Norman Macleod had been down on his hands and knees and counted the ears that came forth from one grain. But Martin also understood that the digging of the ground with a spade and generous dressing with sea-ware were the the key to a successful crop. It was vital also to allow the ground to rest. In North Uist the people showed him how,

> a plot of ground which hath lain unmanured for some years, would in a plentiful season produce fourteen ears of barley from one grain.[10]

This degree of hyperbole relating to the barley crop hides the true difficulties of raising any arable at all in the islands, with a few exceptions that included Canna, Tiree, parts of Skye and Orkney. Pennant, always measured, observed how, in Skye,

> The westerly wind blows here more regularly than any other, and arriving charged with vapour from the vast Atlantic, never fails to dash the clouds it wafts on the lofty summits of the hills of Cuchullin, and their contents deluge the island in a manner unknown in other places ... the rains begin with moderate winds,

> which grow stronger and stronger till the autumnal equinox, when they rage with incredible fury.
>
> The husbandman then sighs over the ruins of his vernal labours; sees his crops fell the injury of climate: some laid prostrate; the more ripe corn shed by the violence of the elements. The poor foresee famine ... the humane tacksmen agonise over distresses. [11]

Bere has a distinctive flavour, being very slightly astringent. A retired school teacher from Wick, Miss Christine Davidson, recorded how,

> My mother regularly made bere-meal porridge - it was more jelly-like than oatmeal porridge. There's an old expression - It's bere-meal tasted - meaning that you were getting the same thing over and over again, and that you were tiring of it. And by the summer time you were fed up with the bere; sometimes it had gone off or was bad with mites. [12]

But she also remembered wafer-thin bere-meal scones cooked by her aunt on a brander; the open-work girdle that hung over the fire. The soft bere-meal scones found in Orkney nowadays incorporating a proportion of wheaten flour and raised with baking powder are a far cry from the old water bannocks. When warm from the fire they made filling food but when cold they soon became hard and heavy.

> Barley cakes, because of their dark colour, were not as popular as oat-cakes, but they had the double advantage of being extremely nourishing and easily carried without crumbling. [13]

Pease flour tended to be baked into a thinner bannock, [14] when baked with oat flour or barley flour it made a *mashlum* bannock, a term which applied to any bread of mixed meal. Hand bannocks were small and quickly shaped. [15] To keep bread fresh, it was buried in the meal kist.

Special celebration bannocks known as Highland Quarter Cakes were baked to mark the passing of the seasons. The Beltane bannock (*bonnach Bealltain*) had a wash of thin batter.

In Mull it was baked with a hole in it and the cows milked through the hole to ensure a future good supply of milk.[16] At Michaelmas a cake known as *Struan Mìcheil,* baked from three grains, oats, bere and rye to signify the Trinity was mixed with sheeps' milk and baked on a lambskin over a fire of oak, rowan or bramble, these being the three mystical woods. Three layers of batter were laid on each side as it cooked. Small *struans* were also made for individuals, incorporating wild honey and fruits such as bilberries or brambles. It was important that the struan should not break in the baking as that would destroy all the good fortune it should bring to the household.[17] Pennant described St.Michael's cake as,

> composed of two pecks of meal, and formed like the quadrant of a circle; it is daubed with milk and eggs, and then placed to harden before the fire.[18]

Salt bannocks were made on Mull for Hallowe'en, which were meant to make young girls dream of the man they would marry.[19] The New Year bannock with caraway seed was cut into a round by removing the centre with a cup and the edges pinched with finger and thumb.[20]

Although by the mid eighteenth century, generally speaking, oats had overtaken bere as the main cereal crop of the islands, there were significant variations. By the time of the New Statistical Account, oatmeal was still a luxury in Skye[21] and in North Uist.

> The ordinary food is potatoes and barley-bread, which are almost exclusively used among the poorer class,[22]

and barley remained a prominent part of the diet into the twentieth century, particularly in Orkney, where it is still sold. Angus Duncan of Scarp remembered bere ground in a hand quern at her door by a widow with five children to feed.[23]

Nutritionally, oatmeal is far richer than bere-meal. While oatmeal has 14-17% protein, barley-meal has just 7-9%. While oatmeal has 6-10% oil, barley-meal has a mere half to 1%. In earliest times there were few named varieties but the different kinds were usually known by their colour. The common oat, known as the black or grey oat, was the most important in the islands. Research indicates that these older varieties of oats, or 'straw types' were higher than modern strains in both protein and oil.[24]

But although bread was a staple and meal paid both rent and wages the islands rarely produced an adequate supply. During the first quarter of the nineteenth century Fair Isle, for example was "supplied chiefly from the mainland,"[25] in spite of good crops. The arable area, although exceptionally well-manured was just inadequate for the population of 250. Orkney was the exception, actually exporting grain to Shetland, Norway and to the mainland.[26] From the mid-eighteenth century there was a steady flow of imported meal into the Hebrides from the south, augmenting, for a rising population, that which could be grown on the thin, coastal soils.[27] But cash had to be found to pay for it, through sales of cattle, fish and produce, or through the kelp industry. On Jura

> In good seasons sufficient bere and oats are raised as will maintain the inhabitants; but they sometimes want, I suppose from the conversion of their grain into whisky ... It is to be feared that their competence of bread is very small.[28]

On Colonsay bere also went as rent for distillation,

> to the very starving of the islanders, who are obliged to import meal for their subsistence.[29]

On Rum,

> so small is the quantity of bere and oats that there is not a fourth part produced to supply their annual wants ... They are a well-made and well-looking race, but carry famine in their aspect. Are often a whole summer without a grain in the island; which they regret, not on their own account, but for the sake of their poor babes.[30]

Throughout the nineteenth century the benevolent societies of the Lowlands and the landlords of the Highlands provided intermittent meal supplies, a task finally centralised in the formation of the Central Board of Management for Highland Relief, set up in response to the horrors of the potato failure of 1846 and 1847.[31]

Oatcakes on the girdle and hardening off, Mingulay, 1904.

During those famine years the Lewis laird, James Matheson, supplied his tenants with meal but added the cost of it to their rent bills, worsening the plight of those already in arrears.

> The quantity of meal which they got on Cr in 1846-&47 and still unpaid is what leaves them so much in debt - the greater number still deny the quantity charged against them and many assent that they paid the meal when they got it to James & John McKenzie Ederoel then ground officers - Neither John nor James can read or write and it was quite impossible they could keep account of the meal given at and from whom they got payment.[32]

There were countless different ways of consuming meal, whether it came from the local economy or from ships sailing out of Peterhead or Aberdeen, in the guise of trade or as famine relief. Brose was made by pouring boiling water over oatmeal and a little salt to be eaten immediately with milk - if available.

> Raw meal brose is much used, but it is said to cause faintness ...

noted a nurse from Lewis in1914.[33] But it had the advantage of quick preparation and left the meal with more bite and texture than does porridge where it is softened in the cooking. Brose avoided the one-third shrinkage observable in porridge as it cools. One of the many Hebridean Christian legends offers an explanation of this phenomenon. Christ and His Mother

> ... entered a house where there was porridge boiling and asked for some. The good-wife refused, saying there was little enough for those who were out ploughing. When they had gone she took off the pot, and began to pour out the porridge, but though there had been plenty, there were now not two bowlfuls left.[34]

Frederick Rea went to South Uist in 1889. He was the first Englishman to be appointed head teacher of Garrynamonie School and his diary shows his fresh approach to all he saw and his good eye for detail. His first breakfast on the island was taken with Father Allan Macdonald (1859-1905) then priest.

> The porridge in soup plates was served first, each plate being accompanied with a large basin of cold milk. This being new in my experience of taking porridge, caused me considerable diffidence; but Father Allan, tactfully ignoring my hesitancy, commenced his portion, while I followed suit, imitating him as well as I could. We had our basins of milk before us, the plate of porridge on the right; a little of the hot porridge was taken in a large spoon which was then dipped into the cold milk, and porridge and milk then placed in the mouth. I am afraid that I

> was rather clumsy at first, letting the porridge slip from the spoon into the basin of milk, and having to fish about for it, or taking too large a portion of hot porridge to be cooled quickly and consequently burning my mouth; but I attained greater dexterity before finishing.[35]

Different methods of drying grain could produce different flavours in bannocks, porridge or broth where grain was used for thickening. *Graddaning* or burning off of the straw was described by Martin Martin, as he observed it in Skye. This method of quickly drying fresh grain produced a toasted or *birstled* flavour, something which islanders much craved.

> They love the graddan, as being more agreeable to their taste.[36]

The method was skilful, but it was also a great waste of straw, which could have been stored as winter feed.[37]

> A woman sitting down takes a handful of corn, holding it by the stalks in her left hand and then sets fire to the ears, which are presently in a flame; she has a stick in her right hand, which she manages very dexterously, beating off the grain at the very instant when the husk is quite burnt; for if she miss of that she must use the kiln, but experience has taught them this art to perfection.

The grain produced in this way would have been hastily ground in a quern, mixed with water, shaped and cooked upon the hearthstone.

> The corn may be so dressed, winnowed, ground, and baked within an hour after reaping from the ground. The oat bread dressed as above is loosening, and that dressed in the kiln astringent, and of greater strength for labourers.[38]

The New Statistical Account refers to the popularity of the graddan, or *min uraraidh*.[39]

> In the twentieth century, on the island of Scarp, still the grain was parched in an ordinary iron pot placed on red-hot cinders beside the fire. It was continuously stirred with a wooden spurtle to prevent burning. The Gaelic name for this process has given writers the word, gradan, as in gradan-bread ...[40]

The flavour of grain in Shetland was also enhanced by roasting. Often in meagre supply *Da Pukkle*[41] when dried in the kettle and ground was known as *bursteen*. The fine meal was dark brown and highly flavoured. Eaten with hot milk it was known as *pramm*.[42] It was made into round cakes, often enriched with butter and baked slowly over the fire. These were called *bursteen brunies*.[43]

Sowens or *soins* in Shetland is an example of the ingenious use of oats. It was a popular everyday dish, refreshing and easily digested as well as being recognised as an important invalid food. A kind of soured *flummery*, sowens was made from the refuse of the grinding process, that is, from the husks of the grains with any adhering fine flour particles. This bran was soaked in cold or warm water, depending on the degree of acidity required. It could take a fortnight in winter or about four days in summer for the floury part to separate out and begin to ferment. By giving it a stir the floury solids were encouraged to the bottom of the tub. When considered ready the thin water on top was poured off and sieved. Fresh water was then poured in and the process repeated until all the flour was separated from the husks. This liquid, *swats* was drunk when milk or ale was short. The sediment was then washed to reduce the acidity and more water added to dilute it to the consistency of thin cream. This could then be par-boiled or boiled until it thickened. When poured into a cool vessel it would set into a creamy-coloured thick jelly to be eaten with milk. Sowens could be stored by drying this residue and cutting it into portions which were then easily re-constituted by adding water or rolled in oatmeal and given to the children as a piece. In Orkney sowens was used to mix scones - giving a pleasantly sour flavour. It has been calculated that 12 ounces of oatmeal make thirteen and a half ounces of hard cakes or 39 ounces of porridge. But the same weight of meal (discounting the three ounces of inedible husk) will made 56 ounces of sowens which may have been more digestible than other forms of meal.[44] What seems certain is that sowens was a comfort food.

> My recollections of sowans

wrote Angus Duncan (1888-1971) from Scarp,

> are that it was greyish in colour, with the consistency of thin porridge without any grains, and that it had a pungent taste.[45]

It was eaten for supper as a change from porridge.

Barley-meal, being drier than oatmeal, made thicker bannocks. Mixing the meal with buttermilk[46] or sowens made them softer than the most simple variety which were mixed with water. Oatmeal could be mixed with barley-meal for bannocks of varying thicknesses. These last became lighter as imported flour and baking soda made their appearance in the islands towards the end of the nineteenth century.

> Bread, the staff of life the world over, was made in large bannocks, whether as scones or oatcakes, on a hanging girdle, fired before an opening made in the peat fire. In the case of oatcakes there was also a quick way of baking it, a small thick bannock being kneaded between the guidewife's palms and fired without bringing the girdle into service. This bannock, usually showing the guidwife's finger marks and in shape resembling a shallow saucer, though larger than a saucer, was known as a *bonnach boiseadh*, or 'palm bannock'.[47]

In Shetland *liver krolls* were a way of flavouring bere with fish; the meal was mixed with cold water into a round cake. A hollow was made in the centre and filled with sillock liver before cooking in the oven or on a brander. It is known that Prince Charles Edward Stewart liked his oatcakes well-fired and flavoured.[48]

In the aftermath of the battle of Culloden (1746) when forced to flee from Lewis to the uninhabited island of Euirn the party took with them in Donald Campbell's boat,

> the head and some pieces of the cow (given to them in Lewis by Lady Killdun) as also two pecks of meal ... they had all along a wooden plate for making their dough for bread, and they made use of stones for birsling their bannocks before the fire.

When Ned Bourke was about to make some bannocks,

> the Prince said he would have a cake of his own contriving, which was to take the brains of the cow and mingle them well in amongst the meal, when making the dough, and this he said they would find to be very wholesome meat.

Donald remembered how he "gave orders to birsle the bannock well ... " When it had been thoroughly cooked and divided among them, "it made very good bread indeed." It must have been a thickish bannock for the brains to be successfully incorporated. There is a certain irony in a letter home written during the very same month, May 1746 by a soldier in Cumberland's victorious army ...

> he (Cumberland) beeing the darling of mankind, for we had certainly been starved had it not been his care to bring ovens and bakers with him.[49]

Towards the end of the nineteenth century shop bread from Glasgow became available but baking[50] remained an important activity for the housewife. In Rum,

> the Post Office sold the bare necessities for existence, such as bread and large sea-biscuits. We very rarely bought bread, and if we did, treated it as a luxury, and as a special treat were given half a slice on Sundays. All our scones, oatcakes and barley bannocks were made at home, a week`s supply at one big baking.[51]

In Lewis, however, where the pressure of population on the land was greatest, native produce had yielded to imported articles.

> There the home-made barley bannocks have in a large measure been supplanted by loaf bread.[52]

References — chapter 1

1. *Monro's Western Isles of Scotland,* ed. R. W. Monro, Edinburgh 1961 p.42
2. *Scottish National Dictionary*
3. *Ibid.*
4. Mitchell, Arthur, *The Past in the Present*, Edinburgh 1880 p.74
5. Pennant, Thomas, *A Tour in Scotland and Voyage to the Hebrides, 1772,* Edinburgh 1998 p.280
6. Miss Joy Sandison of Unst's personal recollections
7. *Adomnan's Life of Columba*, ed. Allan Orr Anderson & Marjorie Ogilvie Anderson, Edinburgh 1961 pp.329-331
8. *OSA*, Vol. X p.350
9. Martin, Martin, *A Description of the Western Isles of Scotland circa 1695*, Edinburgh 1984 p.118
10. *Ibid.*, p.127
11. Pennant, Thomas, *A Tour in Scotland and Voyage to the Hebrides, 1772,* Edinburgh 1998 p.307
12. *Scotland on Sunday*, 25.7.93
13. Macdonald, Donald, *Lewis A History of the Island*, Edinburgh 1978 p.54
14. *Scottish National Dictionary*
15. Buxton, Ben, *Mingulay,* Edinburgh 1995 p.90
16. McNeill, F. Marion, *The Silver Bough*, 4 vols., Glasgow 1959 vol.2 p.67
17. *Ibid.*, pp. 105-106
18. Pennant, Thomas, *A Tour in Scotland and Voyage to the Hebrides, 1772,* Edinburgh 1998 p.272
19. *Tocher* 23, p.28
20. *Tocher* 16, p.324
21. *NSA* Vol.14, p.319
22. *Ibid.*, p.173
23. Duncan, A., ed. *Hebridean Island Memories of Scarp,* Edinburgh 1995 p.90
24. Findlay, W. M., *Oats*, Edinburgh 1956, pp.198,199
25. Scott, Walter, *The Voyage of the Pharos*, Scottish Library Association, 1998 p.37
26. Shaw, F.J., *The Northern and Western Islands of Scotland*, Edinburgh 1980 p.167
27. Gray, Malcolm, *The Highland Economy 1750-1850*, Edinburgh 1956 pp. 42,44
28. Pennant, Thomas, *A Tour in Scotland and Voyage to the Hebrides, 1772,* Edinburgh 1998 p.202
29. *Ibid.*, p.229
30. *Ibid.*, p.277
31. Devine, T. M., *The Great Highland Famine*, Edinburgh 1988 p.123
32. Mackenzie, John Munro, *Diary 1851*, Acair 1994, pp.33,34

33. Mackenzie, W. Leslie ed., *Scottish Mothers and Children*, The Carnegie United Kingdom Trust, Dunfermline 1917 p.448
34. Goodrich Freer, A., *Outer Isles,* London 1902 p.217
35. Rea, F.G., *A School in South Uist,* London 1964 p.9
36. Martin, Martin, *A Description of the Western Isles of Scotland circa 1695,* Edinburgh 1984 pp. 243,244
37. Pennant, Thomas, *A Tour in Scotland and Voyage to the Hebrides, 1772,* Edinburgh 1998 p.279
38. Pennant considered this a ruinous practice, destructive of thatch and manure, but subsequently noting, as if in justification that, "Graddaned corn was the parched corn of Holy Writ."
39. *NSA* Vol.14,p.352
40. Duncan, A., ed. *Hebridean Island Memories of Scarp,* Edinburgh 1995 p.91
41. Saxby, M.R., *Shetland Traditional Lore,* Edinburgh 1932 p.168
"Da Pukkle- is a homely way of referring to the grain, so precious, and such a very uncertain crop in Shetland. The oats, which is known as of Shetland only, is a hard, dark-coloured pukkle with a sort of beard, like barley."
42. Nicolson, James R., *Traditional life in Shetland,* London 1990 p.20
43. Saxby M. R., *Shetland Traditional Lore,* Edinburgh 1932 p.168
44. Fenton, A., Sowens in Scotland, *Folk Life,* vol.12
45. Duncan, A., ed. *Hebridean Island Memories of Scarp,* Edinburgh 1995 p.94
46. Buttermilk makes the lightest scones, cf *The Constance Spry Cookery Book,* London 1972 p.778
47. Duncan, A., ed. *Hebridean Island Memories of Scarp,* Edinburgh 1995 p.94
48. Bishop Forbes, *The Lyon in Mourning,* Edinburgh 1895, 3 vols., vol.1 pp. 169,170
49. *Ibid.*, Appendix A
50. Goodrich Freer, A., *The Outer Isles,* London 1902 p.8
51. Cameron, Archie, *Bare Feet and Tackety Boots,* Luath Press 1988 p.49
52. *Report to the Secretary for Scotland by the Crofters Commission on the social Conditions of the people of Lewis in 1901* p.xcvii

Central hearth, Orkney.

Chapter 2: Pots, Pans and Fireplaces

four thick flags ... (were) ... driven into the ground so as to form a rough kind of square, in the centre of which smouldered a small turf fire. Directly over this, and suspended from the roof-tree, was a long, smoke-blackened chain used for hanging kettles and cooking-pots on.

Kearton. C., *With Nature and a Camera*, London 1897 p.34

A little hole on one side gave an exit to the smoke; the fire is made on the floor beneath; above hangs a rope, with a pot-hook at the end to hold the vessel that contains their hard fare, a little fish, milk, or potatoes.

Pennant, Thomas, *A Tour in Scotland and Voyage to the Hebrides, 1772,* Edinburgh 1998 p.276

The archeological site recently excavated at Kinloch, Rum has provided the earliest certain evidence to date for human settlement in the islands, and indeed, in Scotland. People arrived on these long coasts soon after the last glaciation, about 9,000 years ago. For 4,000 years they lived by hunting, fishing and gathering, until in time turning to agriculture and more permanent settlement.[1] It is possible that the three continuous stone construction rings discovered by archeologists in Jura and containing a base of charcoal, flint objects, hazelnut shells, chips of bone and the remains of limpets, marks a mesolithic hearth site. The men who crouched around this fireplace had probably paddled over from the mainland for autumn hunting of the deer and the seal. Other traces of their hearth have been found, one built in the shelter of three upstanding stones.[2]

The central hearth, direct descendant of those Stone Age fires, survived in the Hebrides into the twentieth century. In her 1803 Journal, Dorothy Wordsworth left an engaging description of one she happened to glimpse during her travels in Scotland. Ironically it was the shortcomings of the breakfast provided in the parlour of the inn at Inveroran - inedible butter, fusty barley cakes, rock-hard oat bread and overboiled eggs that drove her into the kitchen. There was no bell to summon a servant, but when she gingerly opened the door, she saw,

> About seven or eight travellers, probably drovers, with as many dogs, (they) were sitting in a complete circle round a large peat-fire in the middle of the floor, each with a mess of porridge, in a wooden vessel, upon his knee: a pot suspended from one of the black beams, was boiling on the fire; two or three women pursuing their household business on the outside of the circle, children playing on the floor. There was nothing uncomfortable in this confusion: happy, busy or vacant faces, all looked pleasant; and

> even the smoky air, being a sort of natural indoor atmosphere of Scotland, served only to give a softening, I may say harmony, to the whole.[3]

About fifty years earlier, Prince Charles Edward Stewart had drawn less comfort from a central hearth. Soon after his initial landing in Scotland he was entertained in an Eriskay house, where the unfamiliar smoke drove him at regular intervals to duck under and out of the door for a gulp of fresh air. Seating around such a fire consisted of low stools or peats set one on top of another. Had there been a chair of any size in the house - perhaps one fashioned from driftwood, it would have been allotted to this important guest. He was anyway tall. Perhaps the unfortunate Prince's head was fixed in the smoky atmosphere of the higher reaches while his companions were enjoying the glow below the mirk. His fidgeting dismayed his host.

> What a plague is the matter with that fellow, that he can neither sit nor stand still, and neither keep within nor without doors?[4]

The central hearth endured into the twentieth century and can still be seen on museum sites and in conserved buildings. At the Highland Folk Museum, the Highland Vernacular Buildings Trust are re-creating a traditional highland township of turf and stone thatched houses, with replica furnishings and central hearths where the peat smoke hovers beside the box beds and winds its way out of a hole in the thatch. All household cooking took place in the heat of that fire and peat was its traditional fuel.

Peat is not synonymous with the islands. Heskir, Muck and Tiree have none. There they burnt dried horse and cow dung and seaweed - products more properly put to enriching the soil. Where peat was absent or had been used up, turfs were cut from shallow moors, seriously impoverishing the land. Sir Walter Scott, aboard the *Pharos* in 1814 as a guest of the Commissioners of the *Northern Lights*, found it execrable in Orkney,

> the mode of using these extensive commons, where they tear up, without remorse, the turf of the finest pasture, in order to make fuel ...[5]

In Barra and Eriskay the peat had to be carried from areas remote from the settlements. In North Rona and the Skerries the people combed the beaches for the valuable driftwood brought in by the tides. [6] Sometimes a lack of peat meant the need to make long and dangerous sea voyages. The men of North Ronaldsay in Orkney went to Eday for peat. This involved a fourteen mile journey in open boats; a severe prelude to the opening of banks, the cutting and the stacking. They were in fact particularly good peats and by the end of the nineteenth century were in demand from distilleries in the south. [7] In Shetland the residents of the Skerries crossed to the neighbouring island of Whalsay for their peat. The six-mile passage was a dangerous one.[8]

Lewis and the Uists are particularly rich in peat and the immense stacks by the houses are a tribute to community effort.

> Dried peat is a good quiet fuel, but it exacts an immense toll of labour

observed Frank Fraser Darling (1903-1979)[9] who was no shirker himself. A household of four was calculated to need 15,000-18,000 peats to see them through a year for all their heating and cooking. This represents 15-18 full man-days for cutting, not to mention the labour of the women in lifting and stacking, and all to be done at the driest time of the year when the arable ground required preparation.

> The small tenants are employed every hour they can spare ... in furnishing themselves with peats; and after all they can do, they seldom have but a scanty supply of that necessary article. In very rainy seasons, such as the year 1790, there has been such a scarcity of fuel as to oblige people to go with their horses several miles for heath to dress their victuals with.[10]

Peat is a fuel produced by bad drainage and a cool climate. The essential condition of its formation is that vegetable remains are laid down at a rate exceeding that of their decomposition. In the larger, well-endowed islands the right to cut was synonymous with rights over the common moor. Some landlords, even before the eighteenth century, hedged it round with restrictions, aiming to conserve stocks where they were limited. The tacksmen and richer farmers of the Northern Isles paid others to cut peats for them.[11]

A long, open, peat bank is a beautiful sight, especially when cutting is in progress. There is a certain rhythm in one man cutting, another taking the peat from the blade, a third setting it up into a little heap of three or four to best expose it to the drying winds. And at the end of the bank a fire from last year's long dry peats, brought up from the house stack to make a fire to boil an old black kettle for tea and comfort.

Peat burns slowly, generating a sweet-smelling smoke and very little residue. For these reasons, it is particularly well-suited to the floor-level central hearth. The smoke-impregnated thatch was a valuable resource removed annually to manure the field.

> It is to this purpose that the eyes and lungs both of children and adults are sacrificed.[12]

Incidence of respiratory disease was high.[13] In Skye, where there was no 'proper chimney accommodation' the parish medical officer noted that,

> conjunctivitis and corneitis are frequent and are greatly aggravated by the peat smoke.[14]

With a similar compassion, Pennant in recording the state of the Jura houses, noted how,

> a pothook hangs over a grateless fire, filled with fare that may rather be called a permission to exist, than a support of vigorous life; the inmates, as may be expected, lean, withered, dusky and smoke-dried. But my picture is not of this island only.[15]

In the Northern Isles the lum was protected on the outside by a movable board, in Shetland known as a *skyle*. It could be adjusted by means of a pole - *skylin da lum* - so that the opening faced away from the wind. The chain or links that held the pot – in Gaelic, the *slabhraidh* – was fixed to a cross-beam and the pot or kettle could be raised or lowered on the chain by means of the crook, sometimes an S shaped piece of iron which hooked onto the pot handle and into the chain.[16]

Slowly and patchily the fireplace evolved and where houses were rebuilt there were refinements. The pot-chain could be replaced by the *swee*, a fixed iron bar from which a small crane swung the pot over or away from the fire.[17]

> Our fireplace is a natural gem, just an open hearth with two stone hobs, so impossible to keep clean that we never try.[18]

His treasure seems to have been a descendant of the early improved hearths built against a partition wall within the house where that existed. The raising of the fire by means of an iron grate, locally made, the large hoods which formed hanging chimneys - of which a nice example can be seen at the Highland Folk Museum at Kingussie - and the eventual development of the gable-end chimney were all important improvements, occurring in different areas at different periods.

Today a Rayburn or Esse cooker, peat-fired, is common in the islands, but the closed oven was not a traditional feature of island cooking. The kettle, cooking pot or girdle was suspended over the fire, a cooking method which more than anything defined the sort of bread, porridge, soups and stews which characterized traditional eating in these areas. The ever-present, ever-boiling kettle probably went some way to institutionalize tea-drinking during the second part of the nineteenth century.

> I agree we consume a lot of tea and sugar, more than we are fit to purchase.[19]

Compared with coal or wood peat is remarkably slow burning and readily revived, hence the ever-burning fire which, most common in the West, so struck visitors to the islands.

> The peat fire in the kitchen had never been extinguished since I had first arrived,

observed John Rea, the gentle schoolmaster at Garrynamonie, South Uist (1890-1894) and a native of Birmingham,

> ... and my sister was most interested in the setting of it for the night. A piece of glowing peat was taken from the centre of the fire and pushed deep into the ash under the grate; two large dampish pieces of peat were then pressed down on this and the fire was set for the night. In the morning the whole would be redly smouldering, and it was only the work of a moment to put the glowing pieces into the grate with the tongs, then a few dry peat pieces on this, then with a puff there was a fire ready for cooking breakfast.

In his schoolroom there were large open fireplaces.

> It appeared that each child was expected to bring to school each morning a piece of peat which should last through the day as the winter days were short.

It must have been one of his assistants who kindled the fire daily, where later he and his mother would make soup in order to provide a mid-day meal for children whom he discovered, to his consternation, ate nothing beween leaving home in the morning and returning after school.[20]

For travellers benighted on the hill or cooking in the open, heather, if it can be found, makes a good fire; especially the dark, dry remnants of last year's growth. A fascinating description of such a picnic, certainly on the grand scale, has been left by John Knox, who was sent to Scotland by the British Fisheries Society in 1786 to investigate the potential for proper development of fishing. During his visit to Stornoway he was entertained by the Earl of Seaforth. Weighed down with equipment and provisions they took to a boat on Loch Roag where, appropriately, they immediately caught some lyth. Stomachs rumbled and a meal seemed in order, so the party landed on one of the loch's many heather-covered little islands. A heather fire was lit in the shelter of a small rock which blazed well and Seaforth himself prepared the fish and and put them into the kettle. Alongside many other imported delicacies, slices of a salmon from freshly-caught fish weighing about half a pound were wrapped in paper and cooked to everyone's satisfaction. The heather fire needed constant feeding by the boatmen, but it cooked effectively.[21]

If signs of a fire show that men have passed by, a quern shows that they have stayed; straddling the work of the land and the preparation of food.

> They grind their oats with a quern, or hand-mill

observed Dr. Johnson in the year 1773,

> ... which consists of two stones, about a foot and a half in diameter; the lower is a little convex, to which the concavity of the upper must be fitted. In the middle of the upper stone is a round hole, and on one side is a long handle. The grinder sheds the corn gradually into the hole with one hand, and works the handle round with the other, the corn slides down the convexity of the lower stone, and by the motion of the upper is ground in its passage.[22]

Such querns had arrived before the Romans and survived into the twentieth century.[23] In the 1876 Rhind lectures Dr. Arthur Mitchell drew the attention of his audience to the fact that querns, although items of great antiquity, were still in common use.

> They are most numerous perhaps in Shetland, but they are common in the Orkney and Hebridean Islands ... there are not only thousands of people in Scotland who still use querns, but there are people who earn part of their livelihood by making and selling them. One man in Shetland, who thus occupied himself, I visited; and I found the selling price of a quern to be from 3s. 6d to 5s. This price is lower than it is believed to have once been, because querns are now more rudely and more coarsely made than they were of old ... only the poorer people are now the purchasers.[24]

Even simpler, the *knockin stane* was just a lump of rough stone, hollowed out so that small amounts of bere could be pounded with another stone or mell.[25]

After the quern, the fire-tongs were one of the most symbolic and valuable items of household equipment. They were blacksmith-made and essential for tending the fire.

> When the bride was brought home ... her husband handed her the tongs as a symbol that he made her the mistress of his house.[26]

Although food could be and was, in early times, cooked in skins,[27] by the sixteenth century it seems that even the poorest had a cooking pot. Martin notes that in St. Kilda the individual provider of a pot for communal use was paid a rent called the pot penny.

> When they go to the lesser isles and rocks to bring home sheep, or any other purchase, they carry an iron pot with them, and each family furnishes one by turns.[28]

Large pots were particularly prized for washing and dying.

> From Shetland there is court case of 1612 brought by Gilbert Moncrieff in Brebister for the return of a nine-gallon cauldron borrowed by Harry Cheyne of Stapness in May 1610 'for brewing of aill to his peat casteris.'[29]

This was a valuable item well worth going to law for.

Those attempting to protect Prince Charles Edward Stewart from his pursuers did not forget this vital utensil, even when aboard ship.

> Donald took care to buy a pot for boyling pottage or the like when they should happen to come to land, and a poor firlot of meal was all the provision he could make out to take with them.[30]

Cooking methods were well-adapted to a situation where it was customary to own only a single cooking pot; fish, for example, was laid over the potatoes and cooked partly in their heat.

Since earliest times iron had been locally smelted; the process was charcoal or, in places, peat-fuelled. Between 1727 and 1736 there was smelting at Invergarry and from 1753 a works at Taynuilt; offshoots of English firms who brought their business nearer Scottish forests in order to source timber for charcoal-making. While smelting was something of a rural cottage industry simple iron pots for porridge and broth stood on a type of base. The slightly narrowed neck and lip made it possible to attach the pot chain or (for the poorest households) a rope collar.[31] Later pots had wooden lids and detachable handles sometimes known as *bools*[32] and either three or four feet which meant the housewife could set them in the fire, cover them with ash and bake meat - making a form of Dutch oven. The Highland Folk Museum at Kingussie has some examples.

When Abraham Darby began to smelt iron with coke it became possible to move the industry away from the traditional forest locations and towards coal and ironstone deposits. It was the Carron ironworks, established in 1759 in Fife which pioneered this new process in Scotland.

> From the outset Carron Company produced a bewildering variety of goods. Plough plates, axle bushes, pots and pans came first.[33]

Carron greatly expanded the range of iron goods available to the poorest households. Part of their success was undoubtedly in their marketing. During the last four decades of the eighteenth century the company's travelling salesmen began to comb the country for buyers, making numerous journeys to the north of Scotland. Later, Carron goods went out from their Glasgow warehouse in ships employed to return with a cargo of kelp from the islands. They carried pots and kettles from one to twenty gallons and priced at a sliding scale of seven pence a gallon. When kelp was booming - between 1790 and 1820 - cash was available for the islanders to buy in these products, such as kettles, and *girdles* - narrow bands of iron bent into a circle with a large oval handle for suspending - and the great variety of decorative bannock spades used for lifting the finished scones and pancakes. This money economy was not universal; some poor people continued to bake their bannocks on a stone.

Given a fundamental shortage of metal goods, wood, horn and heather filled the gap. Baskets of all types and shapes had many uses. In Jura Pennant saw, in a shieling hut,

> pendent shelves made of basket work, to hold the cheese.[34]

Staved vessels were used for pickling. In Shetland there was a high hooped vessel for holding milk ready for churning known as a *span* and a wooden tub-shaped vessel for holding run milk called a *remikel.*[35] Carved wooden spoons and ladles were fashioned at home, plates and quaichs of all sizes carved from solid pieces of wood. In the half underground dwellings used by the St. Kildans on Borrera as temporary shelters,

> a young man pulled an old worm-eaten wooden ladle from a hole in the wall, and explained it was used for dividing porridge amongst those who came to work on the island for a while. The condition of the utensil did not set me longing madly after Borrera porridge.[36]

Clearly this was a badly neglected example, but in general heather pot scrubbers were used for cleaning and there is every reason to suppose that particularly in a dairying society vessels were of necessity well scrubbed.

All available materials of the country were put to ingenious use. In the collections at the Kingussie Folk Museum, founded by Dr. I.F. Grant (1887-1993) can be seen a very unusual brush made from moss, a cream skimmer made from a scallop shell[37] and whisks for frothing milk made from horse-hair. As potatoes became an important part of the diet wooden mashers became widespread. Dr. Grant, who collected widely, recorded

> A dish with the sides of wood and the bottom of wickerwork has several times been described to me as usual in the old days on the west coast and in the Islands. It was used for serving potatoes, with perhaps a relish of herrings. The potatoes were tipped into it from the cooking pot and the water they had been boiled in was allowed to run on to a bundle of fodder, which served as a nourishing bite for any cow that needed special attention.[38]

It is likely that this was just one of a wide variety of fragile domestic items that have not survived. For the serving of food in Lewis the contents of the cooking pot were emptied onto a wooden *clar*,

> a tray, between three or four feet long, about eighteen inches wide, with sides three inches high, sometimes hollowed out of a thick slab of wood. The clar was lined with straw or grass, and after the meal, this juicy bedding was fed to the cows along with any leftovers[39]

Sieves were made by stretching sheepskin over wooden hoops and piercing it through with straightened out fish hooks. A similar implement, unpierced, was used for cleaning meal after grinding, known in Shetland as *da blinnd sieve.*[40]

Some household utensils were provided by the Tinkers, or travelling people, who had important craft skills such as hornworking which were indispensable until the mid-19th century.[41] They made pots and pans, fashioned lamps and did general smithying from their portable forges. During the early twentieth century, while the island of Rum was run as a deer forest, the sea-tinkers came regularly to pick up antlers, cast in April.

> In return ... we were given 'Toby Jugs' and beautifully hand-painted plates.[42]

Long before these tinker acquisitions, or blue and white pottery from Prestonpans or the plates and jugs made by Bell of Glasgow appeared on island dressers a native pottery existed which has come to be known as Barvas Ware.

> We found a lot of fragments of earthenware vessels half an inch thick, and so blackened on the outsides as to lead us to suppose they had been placed on a fire for cooking purposes,[43]

noted Richard Kearton. They were in all probability island made. Such vessels were manufactured and used all over the Western Isles of Scotland from a very early period down to the time when the steamers brought Staffordshire ware into fashion. A dairying economy in particular requires containers of all sorts and in the islands this need was satisfied from local deposits of clay. Dr Arthur Mitchell travelled widely in in the Northern and Western Isles and, in the contempory atmosphere of burgeoning interest in archeology and anthropology became absorbed by what he came to perceive as remnants of the past in the present.

As the Rhind lecturer to the Society of Antiquaries in 1876, he described a visit to the Island of Lewis, thirteen years earlier.

> In driving from Uig to the village of Barvas on the west coast, we passed a stone-breaker sitting at the roadside eating his dinner out of a vessel which struck us as remarkable. We found it, on closer examination, to be even a stranger thing than it seemed to us, as we first caught sight of it. We waited till the stone-breaker had eaten its contents, and then we carried it off; but we had acquired little information regarding its history, because the stone-breaker and we had no language in common. Before reaching Barvas we had a detour to make and some business to transact. When we got there, we found that our acquaintance of the roadside had preceded us. He had hurried home to tell of the profitable sale he had made, and while our horse was feeding, we were visited by many people carrying vessels like the one we had bought, and offering them for sale. They are called Craggans, and we learned that, at a period by no means remote, they had been made in many villages of the Lewis, though at the time of our visit their manufacture was chiefly, if not entirely, confined to Barvas.[44]

Recent research has shown that the manufacture of this ware remained the same from the seventeenth to the twentieth century. It was made by women. The clay was dug by hand and kneaded until soft enough to work into a shape. Then the vessels were formed either on a piece of board or on the ground. When the desired shape had been achieved the piece was left to dry out either in the sun or near the fire. A simple kiln was made by placing the pot in the fire and filling it with burning peat. When the pot was very hot it was moved from the fire and fresh, skimmed milk poured over to create a type of waxy glaze.

Most of the pots seem to have been globular with a narrow neck and mouth - it was said that the opening would take a woman's hand but not the muzzle of a cow or a calf. One dated 1886 at the Highland Folk Museum, Kingussie confirms this description. Craggans were used for water, milk and ale and there is evidence in Skye for vessels with a 3-4 gallon capacity used for storing fish oil. [45] Although their bases were generally curved they could be set up among the smouldering peats and food allowed to cook inside them.

There are interesting examples of teasets, [46] made from about 1880 in imitation of the commercial lowland pottery that had begun to adorn the central feature of many a Highland home, the dresser. Seasonal work in the south and the growth of the fishing industry served to stimulate an increasingly cash-based economy. Willow pattern plates, Baltic bowls and glazed pottery found its way to the islands, to be displayed on dressers sometimes made from driftwood.

> Most Highland dressers are of the open rather than the enclosed variety. The base unit comprises a work surface underhung by a drawer or drawers, with the remainder of the space forming a storage area for pots and other cooking equipment ... the absence of hearth ovens, and, indeed, the survival of the central hearth until well into the nineteenth century meant that most food was cooked by boiling in an iron pot hung over a peat fire, or baked/grilled on a girdle. These utensils, together with large iron kettles, were of an awkward shape and often rather dirty, and the potboard of the dresser must have proved a boon. [47]

References — chapter 2

1. Wickham-Jones, C., The Early Greens, in *Highland Land Use*, ed. Bachell, A., Nature Conservancy Council 1991 Fort William pp.3-7
2. Mercer, John, *Hebridean Islands*, Glasgow and London 1974 p.55
3. Wordsworth, Dorothy, *Recollections of a Tour made in Scotland, 1803* ed. Shairp, J.C Edinburgh 1874 p.183
4. Bishop Forbes, *The Lyon in Mourning*, Edinburgh 1895, 3 vols., vol.1 p.289
5. Scott, Walter, *The Voyage of the Pharos*, Scottish Library Association 1998 p.61 p.61
6. Robson, M., *Rona, The Distant Island,* Acair 1991 p.30
7. Cameron, A.D., *Go Listen to the Crofters*, Acair 1986 p.100
8. Shaw, Frances, J., *The Northern and Western Islands of Scotland,* Edinburgh 1980 p.131
9. Fraser Darling, Frank, *West Highland Survey*, Oxford 1956 p.300
10. *OSA vol. XX p.116*
11. Shaw, Frances J., *The Northern and Western Islands of Scotland*, Edinburgh 1980 p.131 For a full account of peat as a fuel, see Bjorling, P. R. and Gissing, F. T., *Peat, its Use and Manufacture*, London 1907
12. Mackenzie, W. Leslie, *Scottish Mothers and Children*, The Carnegie United Kingdom Trust, Dunfermline 1917 p.427
13. *Ibid.*, p.435
14. *Ibid.*, pp.492,493
15. Pennant, Thomas, *A Tour in Scotland and Voyage to the Hebrides* 1772, Edinburgh 1998 p.217
16. Nicolson, James R., *Traditional Life in Shetland*, London 1990 p.73
17. Grant, I.F., *Highland Folk Ways*, London 1961 p.164
18. Fraser Darling, Frank, *Island Years*, London 1944 p.5
19. Cameron, A. D., *Go, Listen to the Crofters*, Acair 1986 p.80
20. Rea, F. G., *A School in South Uist*, ed. Campbell, J. L., London 1964 p.153
21. Bray, Elizabeth, *The Discovery of the Hebrides, Voyagers to the Western Isles* 1745-1883, London 1986 pp.141-143
22. Johnson and Boswell, *Journey to the Western Islands of Scotland*, Oxford 1930 p.93
23. Duncan, A., ed., *Hebridean Island, Memories of Scarp*. Edinburgh 1995 p.90
24. Mitchell, Arthur, *The Past in the Present*, Edinburgh 1880 p.33
25. Nicolson, James R., *Traditional Life in Shetland*, London 1990 p.78
26. Grant, I. F., *Highland Folk Ways*, London 1961 p.189

27. Monro R. W. ed., *Monro's Western Isles of Scotland*, Edinburgh 1961 p.42, George Buchanan's preface "They boil the flesh with water poured into the paunch or skin of the animal they kill ..."
28. Martin Martin, *A Description of the Western Islands of Scotland, circa 1695* Edinburgh 1994 p.314
29. Shaw, Frances J., The Northern and Western Islands of Scotland, Edinburgh 1980 p.131
30. Bishop Forbes, The Lyon in Mourning, Edinburgh 1895, 3 vols., vol.1 p.163
31. Grant, I.F., *Highland Folk Ways*, London 1961 p.164
32. *Scottish National Dictionary*
33. Campbell, R.H., *Carron Company*, London 1961 p.72
34. Pennant, Thomas, *A Tour in Scotland and Voyage to the Hebrides 1772*, Edinburgh 1998 p.204
35. Nicolson, James R., *Traditional Life in Scotland,* London 1990 p.78p.78
36. Kearton, R., *With Nature and a Camera*, London 1904 p.82
37. Pennant, Thomas, *A Tour in Scotland and Voyage to the Hebrides 1772*, Edinburgh 1998 p.301 "I observe that the great scallop-shell is made use of in the dairies of this country for the skimming of milk. In old times, it had a more honourable place, being admitted into the halls of heroes, and was the cup of of their festivity.
38. Grant, I.F. *Highland Folk Ways* p.188
39. Macdonald, Donald, *Lewis A History of the Island*, Edinburgh 1978 p.54
40. Nicolson, James R., *Traditional Life in Shetland*, London 1990 p.78
41. Highland Folk Museum, Kingussie,
42. Cameron, Archie, *Bare Feet and Tackety Boots*, Luath Press 1992 p.23
43. Kearton, Richard, *With Nature and a Camera*, London 1904 p.14
44. Mitchell, Arthur, The Past in the Present, Edinburgh 1880 pp.25,26
45. *Ibid.*, p.236
46. see National Museums of Scotland, Edinburgh Collections
47. Noble, R., Ross, Highland Dressers and the process of innovation. Reprinted from Regional Furniture, *The Journal of the Regional Furniture Society* 1992 Vol.V p.45

Delving team preparing potato ground, Shetland, 1950s.

Chapter 3: Potatoes, starch and sedition

As time progresses and numbers of men increase, protein gets harder to come by, and the human species has become more and more a direct consumer of carbohydrate ... The more numerous people become the more likely they are to be depressed to the state of being starch-eaters ... starch and sedition go together.

Frank Fraser Darling, 1969 *Reith Lectures* BBC 1970 p.25

> *Perhaps it may seem trifling to mention, that some excellent new potatoes were served up at dinner; but this circumstance, with the forwardness of the hay harvest, shows what may be effected by culture in this island, when the tenure is secure ...*
>
> *Pennant,* Thomas, *A Tour in Scotland and Voyage to the Hebrides, 1772,* Edinburgh 1998, p.211

> In the spring of 1743 Old Clanronald was in Ireland upon a visit to his relatives the MacDonalds of Antrim; he saw with surprise and approbation, the economic practices of the country and having a vessel of his own brought home a large cargo of potatoes.[1]

Neither in South Uist nor in Benbecula were the strange tubers well received. In Stornoway,

> With the utmost difficulty, about forty years ago, the people were prevailed upon to plant potatoes but of which they now plant great quantities, by the plough and by the spade, and find them to be the most useful of all crops raised in the parish.[2]

By the mid-nineteenth century potatoes had become the principal food of a large sector of the population. It is not an exaggeration to say that the potato shaped Highland history. It made possible the survival, and indeed the growth, of a population living in part on some of the most marginal land in Britain.

In Orkney and Shetland potatoes were first grown in the gardens of the big houses and in the outfield on lazy-beds. But by 1790 they had their place in the infield and were being rotated with oats and bere.[3] In Sandwick and Stromness they had become the most important food of the people. Because they could be lifted in August, they filled the hungry gap before the grain harvest which came later than on the mainland. Eaten immediately as they were lifted, without threshing or grinding, they could be cooked with small fish caught from the rocks. As production increased more potatoes were stored for the winter and by the mid nineteenth-century they were commonly part of wages paid in kind to farm servants.

Potatoes were regularly eaten three times a day. For breakfast they would be made into a type of porridge, boiled in their skins, strained, peeled and dried over the fire. A handful of oatmeal and some salt would be sprinkled over and then the mixture mashed and eaten with fresh milk or buttermilk.[4] In the middle of the day the potatoes were again boiled in their skins, put either directly onto the table or into a bowl for hungry workers coming in from the field. Each man peeled his own potatoes with his fingers and dipped them into a bowl of melted fat or butter. And potatoes were baked in the embers of the peat fire, mashed, skins and all and eaten with milk and butter. *Clapshot* - a dish of potatoes and turnips mashed together and eaten with bere bannocks shows how from the earliest times the inhabitants of the Northern Isles were accustomed to a wider range of vegetables than was usual in the Hebrides and were never as similarly reliant on the potato as a subsistence crop.[5]

Ironically, the potato arrived in the Hebrides in the aftermath of the tragedy of Culloden; an agent for survival in an increasingly fractured society. After the Jacobite rising of 1745, the forfeiture of estates and the Disarming Act that followed, a new landlordism emerged in the Highlands. Leases fell to sheep farmers who required and could pay for larger holdings. Meanwhile the people were encouraged to move to the coasts onto marginal land and cut seaweed for the kelp industry. Colonel David Stewart, writing in 1822, noted how,

> ... the aspect of the Highlander, his air, and his carriage, have undergone a marked change ...[6]

The small tenants on new, divided holdings of land were vulnerable. More vulnerable still were cotters with no legal claim to land at all but who in general had possession of a plot on which to grow potatoes, sometimes in exchange for labour on a bigger holding. By the 1840s still,

> the overwhelming majority of the inhabitants depended to a significant extent on smallholdings and tiny patches of land for subsistence.[7]

As the first quarter of the nineteenth century ebbed away so also ebbed the sources of cash for lowland meal. The ending of war in 1815 brought a decline in military employment and a flood of Spanish barilla to destroy demand for kelp. The rigorous labours of the excise men stamped on illicit distilling and even the herring were less, deserting the lochs in the period from 1830.[8]

By the time of the New Statistical Account potato production was standing at 75% of grain production and by the time disease struck the potato was probably forming seven-eighths of the food of the Hebrides.[9] From the 1830s, shortages were endemic to the Hebrides, culminating in the crisis of 1846. When the potato famine struck, it was found that of thirteen districts most reliant on potatoes, nine were in the islands. What seems probable, however, is that although oats and bere continued to dominate as a field crop the potato, though slow to spread, became a universal standby, particularly for the poorest people living upon the poorest land.[10] (In Sleat)

> ... there are 225 families, comprising upwards of 1100 individuals, located in different parts of the parish, who pay no rents, deriving their subsistence from small portions of land given them by the rent-payers for raising potatoes. These are a burden to the proprietor, inasmuch as they destroy the land in cutting fuel and turf; and are a grievous burden to the inhabitants generally, from the extent of pauperism prevailing among them.[11]

The potato is a uniquely nutritious vegetable. 77% of the tuber consists of water, the remaining 23% being about 80-88% starch and 3-6% sugar. The starch is ranked by nutritionists above that of cereals. 2% is nitrogen-containing and a half of that consists of tuberin - the vital protein. One pound of new potatoes a day will provide an adult with adequate vitamin C, although storing and cooking reduce the levels considerably. Vitamins B1 and B2 are there, but not in large amounts. A and D are absent, but they are present in milk, a vital adjunct to a diet of potatoes.[12] These unique qualities, along with ease of cultivation served to suppress social and economic problems of the Hebrides, until disease revealed the weaknesses within.

If you walk the road from Daliburgh to Glendale or from Leverburgh to Rodel you will see the lazy-beds or *feannagan* where the potatoes grow, a dozen rows, perhaps. If it is summer the flowers will be swaying, the shaws lush. Their flavour is remarkable. They grow where there was no soil to nurture them, around the rocks that were too big and heavy to clear. Women and girls carried turves and seaweed in creels to make these beds.

> Nothing can be more moving to the sensitive observer of Hebridean life than these lazybeds of the Bays district of Harris. Some are no bigger than a dining table ... one of these tiny lazybeds will yield a sheaf of oats or a bucket of potatoes, a harvest no man should despise. [13]

The planting of potatoes was first seen as part of a move towards agricultural improvement. The Rev. Walker, who toured the Hebrides and reported on the state of agriculture there in 1764 recommended that the crops grown in the 'infield' be rotated, with green crops, turnips, beans and potatoes. [14]

> It was not till after the year 1770, that my father planted potatoes ... it required some time and persuasion to induce his servants to eat them. [15]

A crop safe beneath the ground, protected from wind and storm, easily harvested and stored had obvious attractions to a people so dependent on what they themselves could produce. Particularly so when the whole summer, from late May to September was taken up with the gathering and burning of seaweed to produce the rich, alkaline ash which meant a small, cash income, and with it the ability to buy in meal.

From the 1830s, a virus affecting the potato crop in other parts of Britain known as the *Curl* began to reduce yield. [16] For the time being, however, the fresh breezes that played around the northern and western coasts seemed to protect the potato, which was by that date a mainstay of the people of the Western Isles. But the reliance upon the single crop carried with it the danger of blight and hunger. From the 1830s, shortages were endemic to the Hebrides, culminating in the crisis of 1846, when three-quarters of the supply was lost through Blight.

Earthing up potatoes on the machair, 1880s.

> In spite of the proprietor`s efforts, the famine years of 1845-50 were difficult for everyone. Not only was there disease in the potatoes, but the grain harvests were also poor, fish was scarce and cattle prices low.[17]

The Rev. Dr. Norman Macleod, (1783-1862), better known as *Caraid nan Gaidheal* (Friend of the Gaels) worked tirelessly in the cause of famine relief, at the same time drawing attention to the wider issues involved.

> Society in the Highlands has for many years been in a very hollow and rotten state,

he thundered at a public meeting in Glasgow to raise money for famine victims.

> The heads of households are frequently separated from their wives and families ... ranging the country in quest of work, their wives performing the work of men and of horses at home; the children often untrained and uneducated; and the country with all this subjected to periodical visits of famine, which humanity shudders to contemplate. Now, I have no hesitation in saying that the facility of raising a crop of potatoes was the prop and stay of this crazy edifice ... and why is it so? Because vast sections of that country have been given in tack to sheep graziers, some of whom pay now from £2000 to £3000 a year of rent, and from these grazings the population has been driven to America and Australia, or what is worse, to a comparatively useless corner of the estate, where they are allowed to build their turf huts in the midst of an uncultivated waste, and seek subsistence as they best may ... [18]

Where the potatoes darkened, rotted and took on the smell of the charnel house,

> The poor and crowded population in the islands of the Western Hebrides, in Lewis, Barra, and Uist, required all the sympathy and aid in their sore distress that could be afforded ... [19]

£100,000 was raised in Glasgow and Edinburgh alone. Indianapolis sent 75 barrels of Indian corn, Cincinnati (Ohio) 137 barrels of flour and Toronto, meal. But the work of distribution - by local committees - was difficult, patchy and contentious, exacerbated by tensions generated in the aftermath of the Disruption of 1843 when the Free Church created an independent hierarchy and parochial organisation. In North Uist the Committee prevented 'anything like starvation' although labour or money were exacted for the relief of the islanders. In contrast,

> The scene of wretchedness which we witnessed, as we entered on the estate of Colonel Gordon, was deplorable, nay, heart-rending. On one beach the whole population of the country seemed to be met, gathering the precious cockles, hundreds of ponies with

> creels - men, women and naked children all at work. We met a crowd of people at the fords. I never witnessed such countenances - starvation on many faces - the children with their melancholy looks, big looking knees, shrivelled legs, hollow eyes, swollen-like bellies - God help them, I never did witness such wretchedness.[20]

Knowing that the store ship would not return for two weeks Macleod, desperate to help, hired a sloop and sent her to Tobermory for meal. In the shop there was nothing to buy but a few bags of bad biscuits. In Barra food arrived from Lochmaddy as he was preaching but in Berneray all was wretchedness, "miserable patches of land, bad crops, bad tillage ... " His tour ended, however, on a note of optimism.

> I have seen all the ministers of the Presbytery of Uist, ascertained the state of the parishes, and am enabled to report the crops admirable. Potatoes, etc., planted, and all looking well.[21]

But for the rest of the century the potato harvest continued to fluctuate and the return could never be relied on. Famine conditions recurred in 1851 and 1856. Osgood Mackenzie (1842-1922) who created the great garden at Inverewe never forgot the scene of deprivation and hovering starvation he witnessed as a boy in a house in Harris. It was 1853, the era of intermittent famine, and he and his mother went into a house to buy milk.

> The good wife, like all the Harris people, had most charming manners, but she was busy preparing the family breakfast, and bade us sit down on little low stools at the fire and wait till she could milk the cows for us. Then occurred a curious scene, such as one could hardly have witnessed elsewhere than in a Kaffir kraal or an Eskimo tent or Red Indian Tepe. There was a big pot hanging by a chain over the peat fire, and a creel heaped up with short heather which the women tear up by the root on the hillsides and with which they bed the cows. The wife took an armful of this heather and deposited it at the feet of the nearest cow, which was tied up within two or three yards of the fire, to form a drainer.

Then, lifting the pot off the fire, she emptied it on to the heather; the hot water disappeared and ran away among the cow`s legs, but the contents of the pot, consisting of potatoes and fish boiled together, remained on top of the heather. Then, from a very black-looking bed three stark naked boys arose one by one, aged, I should say, from six to ten years, and made for the fish and potatoes, each youngster carrying off as much as both his hands could contain. Back they went to their bed, and started devouring their breakfast with apparently great appetites under the blankets! No wonder the bed did not look tempting! We got our milk in course of time, but I do not think it was altogether relished after the scene we had witnessed ... "[22]

Such scenes were all too commonplace during the middle years of the century and there were plenty of people with neither fish nor salt to savour their potatoes. Finally, the effects of the economic recovery of the 1860s and 1870s did trickle down to the crofters; those who were left after famine, evictions and emigration. Cattle prices rose and the stirks that had been worth less than one pound in 1840 were now selling for between six and nine pounds. Sheep too were selling better. There were opportunities for seasonal work on the sheep farms and on sporting estates, now proliferating. But the kelp industry had gone and working away, at the lowland harvest, at the fishings or for girls, in service, became the norm.[23]

The able-bodied among them, after their potatoes are planted in the end of spring, go to the south in search of employment. They return again at Martinmas; and their earnings go to pay the landlord`s rents and to support the weaker members of their families ... there is great poverty and privation ... their food consists principally of potatoes."[24]

Where communications and markets were still in their infancy, incoming cash could not remove or reduce the desire and need for land on which to grow food, and most especially potatoes.

> The Eriskay cottar, it may be remarked, earns as much money by the fishing as the crofter does, but the want of home produce is a great hardship to him. There is no local market where he can buy milk, for instance, and if he has not a cow feeding on his neighbours' land he has either to beg for milk or do without it. He is in a like position as regards the matter of potato ground.[25]

Cottars in Barra told the Napier Commission that the crofters exacted 60 days' labour in lieu of rent for their potato ground which did not anyway give a particularly good return. Michael Buchanan of Borve, Barra, described how,

> Each person takes the planting of a barrel of potatoes, and we calculate an acre to plant about eight barrels ... the return we get from one barrel is eight barrels, or ten or twelve in a good year, and some years hardly double the seed we put in.[26]

This most vulnerable section of society, lacking even a potato patch sometimes took desperate action. Hence the report that

> " ... Some of the squatters have cultivated pieces of moorland."[27]

References — chapter 3

1. Walker, John, *Economic History of the Hebrides*, Edinburgh 1808 2 vols. vol.1 p.251
2. *OSA*, Vol., X1X p.249
3. Scott, Walter, *The Voyage of the Pharos*, Scottish Library Association 1998 p.61
4. Fenton, Alexander, *The Northern Isles*, Edinburgh 1978 pp.419,420.
5. Salaman, Redcliffe N., *The History and Social Influence of the Potato*, Cambridge 1989 p.381
6. Stewart, Col. David, *Sketches of the Character, Manners and Present State of the Highlanders of Scotland*, Edinburgh 1822 2vols., vol.1 p.132
7. Devine, T. M., *The Great Highland Famine,* Edinburgh 1988. pp.3,4
8. *Ibid.*, p.11
9. Salaman, Redcliffe N., *The History and Social Influence of the Potato,* Cambridge 1989 p.374
10. Gray, Malcolm, *The Highland Economy*, 1750-1850 Edinburgh 1956, p.34
11. *NSA* Vol.14 p.319
12. Salaman, Redcliffe N., *The History and Social Influence of the Potato*, Cambridge 1989 pp.122,123
13. Fraser Darling, Frank, *West Highland Survey*, Oxford 1956 p.44
14. Walker, John, *Report on the Hebrides 1764 and 1771* ed. McKay, Margaret M., Edinburgh 1980 p.15
15. Stewart, Col. David, *Sketches of the Character, Manners and Present State of the Highlanders of Scotland,* Edinburgh 2 vols., vol.1 p.142
16. Salaman, Redcliffe N., *The History and Social Influence of the Potato*, Cambridge 1989 p.367
17. Macdonald, Donald, *Lewis A History of the Island*, Edinburgh 1978 p.40
18. *Memorials of Rev. Norman Macleod* Edinburgh 1888 pp.219,220
19. *Ibid.*, p.225
20. *Ibid.*, pp.231,232
21. *Ibid.*, p.240
22. Mackenzie, Osgood Hanbury, *A Hundred Years in the Highlands,* Edinburgh1998 p.86
23. Hunter, James, *The Making of the Crofting Community*, Edinburgh 1976 ch.7
24. *NSA*,Vol.14, p.319
25. *Report to the Secretary of State for Scotland by the Crofters' Commission on the Social Condition of the People of Uist in 1903, as compared with twenty years ago* p.cxix
26. Cameron, A. D., *Go Listen to the Crofters*, Acair 1986 p.21
27. Mackenzie, W. Leslie, *Scottish Mothers And Children*, The Carnegie United Kingdom Trust, Dunfermline 1917 p.477

Ewe milking, St. Kilda, 1896.

Chapter 4: Dairying

The milk cow is the provider of our households, and we are happier ourselves if she is in good order ...

Frank Fraser Darling, *Crofting Agriculture*, Edinburgh 1945 p.131

Now I have no place to tether a cow in, and cannot have a drop of milk.

William Hutcheson, of Whalsay, Shetland, to the Napier Commission, Cameron, A.D., *Go Listen to the Crofters*, Acair, 1986 p.39 [1]

In the penury of these malignant regions, nothing is left that can be converted to food. The goats and the sheep are milked like the cows.

Johnson and Boswell, *Journey to the Western Islands of Scotland*, Oxford 1930 p.74

Where crops were hard to grow the importance of milk in the diet of the islands cannot be underestimated. From earliest times cattle were always the most important source, with sheep and goats also regularly milked. While the milking of sheep declined in the lowlands at the turn of the seventeenth century it remained a dietary feature in the islands for very much longer. The St. Kildans continued to milk their ewes long after they knew it to be unusual.

> ... Although we tried every device to get them to allow my brother to photograph them in the act we failed. They would not permit this to be done for love or money, under the impression that people who saw the picture would laugh at at them. [2]

Sheeps' milk was widely considered to make better cheese, though some found it tasteless. [3] The butter was certainly inferior and often went to be mixed with tar for smearing sheep. For island communities, milk, butter and cheese were especially important during the summer months, when the previous years' meal might be all but exhausted. The small black cattle that in summer were taken to the high grazings and in winter picked over the infield stubble were a form of traditional social security. Gaelic proverbs illustrate how cattle and their milk were greatly valued.

Is fheàrr aon sine na ceathramh coirce - One teat (of a cow) is better than a quarter of oat. And where scarcity hovered - *Is fheàrr aon sine bà na bolla dhen mhin bhàin*- Better one teat of a cow than a boll of Lowland meal. [4]

Before turnip crops were established, the condition of island cattle deteriorated severely over the winter months as a result of a chronic lack of fodder. In his native Skye, Martin Martin noted how,

> the cows ... become mere skeletons in the spring, many of them not being able to rise from the ground without help; but they recover as the season becomes more favourable ...[5]

Pennant found Skye cattle being fed meal and saw how they grazed hungrily on seaweed at low tide.[6] The improvers blamed the practice of graddaning for the lack of feed.[7] Dr. John Walker reports that Sir James Macdonald of Sleat had expressly forbidden the burning of grain on his estates and ordered that all corn should be threshed and kiln dried. By the 1730s some hay was being made in Skye, but only enough to feed the stirks during winter.

> The sowing of Rye Grass and Clover would be the best Remedy for that Scarcity of Winter Provender, which is so fatal to the Cattle in this Country; but the farmers are positive in alledging that these sown Grasses could not be made into Hay because of the Rains. Wind and Rain, and the Badness of the Climate, is the universal Objection over all the Islands, against any Innovation in Husbandry.[8]

Like the inhabitants, Samuel Johnson blamed the weather for the quality of the Skye hay, describing it as a collection of withered stalks without taste or fragrance and believing most English farmers would throw it away.[9] Yet there is evidence that on the land winter feed was a priority. In Harris, where conditions were arguably even more difficult,

> The grass is the main object for which the farmer labours ... to lay in a store of winter provender for his cattle, and to improve their summer pastures,

noted the Rev. John Macleod in the Old Statistical Account.[10] Even in the mid twentieth century, for Fraser Darling another name for 'haymaking' was 'heartbreaking'.

> ... Making hay is the most hazardous task ... on its success or failure depends the number of stock he will be able to keep and whether there will be milk in winter.[11]

Milk was both precious and extremely perishable. There might be a summer glut requiring a busy spurt of butter and cheese-making or a thin time when whatever milk there was needed to be stretched. Martin describes how milk could be increased in volume to feed a maximum number of mouths.

> Oon, which in English signifies froth, is a dish used by several of the islanders ... in time of scarcity, when they want bread ... a quantity of milk or whey is boiled in a pot, and then it is wrought up to the mouth of the pot with a long stick of wood, having a cross at the lower end.[12]

This process was repeated until the milk was finished; the general view being that the whey at the bottom was the best. Goats' milk was treated in the same way, sometimes with a little butter added in times of plenty. Samuel Johnson was offered frothed milk at a farmhouse near Armadale, among other foods in the luxury category - beef collops, ham and a very good bread pudding.

The versatility of milk can best be shown by a glance at the numerous Gaelic expressions which describe it. *Bainne blàth* for warm milk straight from the cow, *bainne binntichte* for curdled milk, *bainne buaile* for fold milk, *bainne buidhe*, milk yielded by a cow during first two days after calving, *bainne enamha*, a fermentation of fresh and butter-milk frothed with a stick, *bainne chaorach*, sheeps' milk, *bainne gamhnaich*, milk of a farrow cow (one with a year-old calf and still being milked), sour milk, *bainne lom*, skimmed milk, *bainne maistridh*, whipped cream or frothed milk, *bainne milis*, sweet milk, *bainne muidh*e, butter-milk and *bainne nois*, beastings, or the first milk after a birth. *Bainne reamhar* is sheep's milk, boiled and curdled and *bainne ùr*, fresh milk. *Bealltainn* means the rich, milk-producing month of May and *bainne-gamhnaich* means literally the yearling's milk, signifying the scanty results yielded by sucking it.[13]

Modern refrigeration and pasteurization has turned the modern palate away from the *bainne goirt*, or sour milk, so very popular in the past. Yet on a hot July day, in the early 1980s, gathering and clipping sheep on Boreray in the Sound of Harris, a man was seen relishing a drink of what was clearly sour milk from an orange squash bottle. In Lewis the warm July weather which so 'deliciously soured the milk and cream' is remembered with pleasure.[14] In Shetland *hungmill* refers to sour cream strained through a cloth of its whey.[15]

It was noted in the nineteeth century that,

> craggans, in consequence of their porousness, generally contain organic matter in a state of putrescence ... as the result of this, when fresh milk is put into a craggan, it soon becomes tainted.[16]

'Tainted' milk may well have been the norm. Arthur Mitchell describes meeting a girl in Lewis, on her way back from the milking.

> On her back she carried a flat, open creel, half filled with weeds, and on these weeds nestled two large globular craggans full of milk, each with its mouth stopped by a handful of freshly pulled grass.[17]

It could reasonably be assumed that by the time she had reached her house, the milk would in some degree, have turned. In Shetland soured milk was known as *strubba*. It was added to sweet milk as a curdling agent, the whole then heated. Young nettles, if put among the milk would cause it to thicken, without rennet, within 10 minutes.[18]

That sense of plenty which a good supply of milk afforded is evident in the account of herding on Scarp by Angus Duncan at the end of last century.

> I need hardly say that anyone meeting our isleswomen returning from the milking in daylight will find his capacity for rich warm milk tested to the full. Once at least my father was caught in this way, and afterwards suffered for it; and I remember the visiting evangelist, Murdo Macleod, having gone out early for a long stroll, playfully holding our milkmaids off with his walking-stick, as they pressed stoup after stoup upon him.[19]

Archie Cameron of Rum, born in 1903, remembers his mother`s reminiscences of the Lewis shielings, where,

> Stories from the elders of the company would enthrall the youngsters as they munched their hard tack of oatcakes and barley bread, thickly coated with their own homemade butter.[20]

But overall, milk was not plentiful, especially in the winter.[21] The position of cottars without grazing rights was particularly unfavourable. Several reporters to the Napier Commission recorded a lack of milk, producing the tragic evidence of how children were fed imported treacle and water where there was none. Michael Buchanan of Borve expressed to the commissioners how,

> a cow is very necessary for milk, where young children are brought up.[22]

In Foula, Shetland

> ... we give the children a little sugar and water instead.[23]

In Lewis

> the cottar population, having no right to keep stock, are, as a rule, without cows and accordingly without milk for their children.[24]

While milk in general satisfied a local need, butter and cheese, from earliest times had been items for rent and export. Before 1800, the people of Shetland and Orkney paid their rents in the poorer 'grease butter' while the good butter was eaten at home. In seventeenth century Mull the standard rental for the joint tenants per pennyland was four stones of butter and four quarts of cheese.[25] Where grain production was small - as in Shetland - the importance of the export of dairy products was greatest, because it meant that cash was available for the buying in of meal. Erasmus Doull of North Roe in Northmavine reported to the Napier Commission that having enough pasture, he sold annually "perhaps twenty pounds of butter at 10d. to 1s. a pound."[26]

Walker describes North Uist as exporting annually 300 stone of butter and 200 of cheese. Butter was selling at six shillings per stone and Cheese at three shillings.

> A good Cow usually produces to the Value of a Guinea in Butter and Cheese from Whitsunday to Martinmass, but the common Practice, is to raise only one Calf upon the Milk of two Cows. These, besides the Milk required to support the Calf, generally produce 3 Stone of Butter, and 6 Stone of Cheese between Whitesunday and Martinmass, which amounts to £1 16sh.[27]

In the mid-nineteenth century the St. Kildans, who did not make butter, (preferring fulmar oil) were each exporting 24 lbs of cheese.[28] Though individual beasts may have been troublesome, the regular task of milking cows was an easy one compared with the work of butter and cheese-making. Hence the proverb - *Is lìonmhor bean-bhleoghainn, ach is tearc banachag* - milking women are plentiful, but dairymaids are rare.[29]

Butter-making, in its simplest form, was laborious. It could take half a day for solid globules to appear out of the milk, which might be fresh or, more likely, have been left to stand. The milk was shaken in a wooden tub or craggan or even in a leather bag. The various finds of 'bog butter' show the extent of the pastoral economy and the extremes that were gone to in ancient times to keep this valuable commodity cool. It was probably as much a currency as a food. Indeed, it is striking that butter was the one food item that Charles Edward Stuart was rarely without while being hunted after the battle of Culloden. Ned Bourk, camping with the Prince on the island of Euirn, twelve miles from Stornoway was concerned by scraps of bread that had got mixed up in it, as he had carried it between two fardles or oatcakes.

> Donald Macleod, looking at the butter, said the deel a drap of that butter he would take, for it was neither good nor clean.

Finally they were persuaded by the Prince that the butter "will do exceedingly well." The incident serves to show that butter could be dirty, but when good and available it was used lavishly.

> They made a very hearty meal of the fish and the crumbs swimming among the butter.[30]

Plunge churns, which comprised a staved, wooden cylinder and plunger with a cross-shaped or rounded and pierced head did not reach the islands until the nineteenth century. In Orkney and Shetland the milk was allowed to stand until it thickened naturally before churning began. After the butter was removed from the churn for washing, salting and patting, boiling water was poured onto the remaining buttermilk. This then separated and could be strained - the solids making a kind of soft cheese known as kirn milk and the fluid a refreshing drink known as *blaand*.[31] The first milk of a cow after calving was known as beest milk and a Shetland cookery book recommends adding a little water to it, as it is very strong.[32] Beest could also be made into kloks by baking in the oven until thick and set.[33]

Where the system of shielings operated, there is no doubt that the summer butter and cheesemaking was a time of great pleasure. Cattle were transferred to the higher or more remote ground where the grazing was best and where a good supply of water eased the cleaning of vessels. There women and children lived in temporary huts, herding, milking, churning and cheesemaking. A first hand account of Lewis shielings, describes how,

> the milk was allowed to lie in basins for a couple of days before the cream was skimmed. This operation took place morning and evening, and when a sufficient amount of cream was collected this was put into a churn and turned into butter. The buttermilk was greatly appreciated by the herds and calves and by the milk-maids for baking. A calf's stomach usually hung from a rafter where milk, mixed with salt, and dried, was used as rennet to thicken the milk if necessary. This thick milk was placed in a pot over a slow fire and brought to a certain temperature, not unlike that of a baby's bath. It was never allowed to boil or the curds would become hard. The white curds, *crowdie*, were then squeezed to drive out the whey and some salt added, and placed in a wooden vat called a *fiodhan* where they were left under pressure until they became cheese, which was then hung from a rope to finish the drying properly. The whey was as greatly appreciated as the buttermilk.[34]

The shieling system served a double purpose, because once the crops were beginning to sprout, around late May, it was imperative to keep the cattle away from the infield. In the Northern Isles, tethering served the same function. In Scarp Angus Duncan, from his own herding days, knew the remains of the old shieling huts. Some of them had enough of their thick walls standing to show the recesses where in a previous generation the milk basins had been set out. Wooden milkpails with Sunday milkings were still being left on these shelves at the end of last century as no milk was carried home on a Sunday.

It seems likely that most of the cheese made for domestic consumption was of the soft type, was unsalted until the later period and was made from a wide variety of combinations of fresh or soured, skimmed or fresh milk. Samuel Johnson noted the different preparations of milk brought to the table in the Western Isles. Crowdie, as described by Donald Macdonald (1904-1990) could be mixed with butter or cream for a rich variant. It holds a special place as the comfort food of the Hebrides.

CROWDIE

Ingredients
A basin of thick milk

Method

Take the milk and put it beside the fire until it warms up slowly.
(Today, you can put it on the side of a stove, if there isn't a big fire on).
As it warms it changes into crowdie and whey.
When it is ready, sieve the whey off it, and leave the crowdie in the sieve to dry a little.
Make it into a cheese round.

How to eat

Eat this with fresh butter on scones, oatcakes or barley cakes.
If you are rich, or if you have a good cow, mix cream with it, and you will enjoy it as the greatest delicacy you've ever eaten.

(From *Annlan is Eile*, a book of traditional dishes collected by Catrìona Dunn and a group of girls from the Nicolson Institute, 1978.)

Where salt was in short supply the ash from seaweed or straw was used to flavour cheeses.[35]

> ... See on the Jura side some sheelins or summer huts for goatherds, who keep here a flock of eighty for the sake of the milk and cheese. The last are made without salt, which they receive afterwards from the ashes of sea-tang, and the tang itself which the natives lap it in.[36]

However, there was also harder cheese made in small quantities, a slice of which was dry enough to bear a weight of oatmeal. Prince Charles Edward Stuart, pursued in the hills of Lochaber after the battle of Culloden, and desperately short of rations, was fortunate enough to come upon some

> shealing huts where they expected to meet some people.

But there was no-one there. Lieutenant MacDonald, the brother of MacDonald of Glenaladale, knowing the country well, was sent off to find food. He came back after some hours,

> having got only two small cheeses, that would not be a morsel to the piece of them.[37]

The Prince, arriving in relative safety at Corriscorridill,

> where having chosen a fast place they took such refreshment as the exigency of the time afforded them, his royal highness covering a slice of cheese with oatmeal, which, though but dry fare, he ate very comfortably ...[38]

By the nineteenth century, hard cheese was made by wrapping the curd in a cloth and putting it in

> a cheeser, a round staved vessel with a partition with many holes bored in it about two-thirds of the way down. A heavy stone was put on top and the whey drained away through the holes.[39]

Equipment of this type probably came late to the islands. Milk skimmers made from shells show the extent to which local materials were put to use.

As a food, cheese was highly prized - as the saying goes, *tha thu cho sona 's ged an robh clach ad chàbaig* - you are as happy as if your cheese weighed a stone.

References — chapter 4

1. In 1883 Gladstone's Liberal Government set up a Royal Commission chaired by Lord Napier to enquire into the condition of the crofters and cottars in the Highlands and Islands of Scotland.
2. Kearton, R., *With Nature and a Camera*, London 1904 p.19
3. *Ibid.*, p.39
4. *Gaelic Proverbs*, ed. Nicolson, Alexander, Edinburgh 1996
5. Martin, Martin, *A Description of the Western Isles of Scotland circa 1695*, Edinburgh 1984 pp.207,208
6. Pennant, Thomas, *A Tour in Scotland and Voyage to the Hebrides, 1772,* Edinburgh 1998 p.310
7. Walker, Dr. John, ed. Mackay, M.M., *Report on the Hebrides of 1764 and 1771*, Edinburgh 1980 p.209
8. *Ibid.*, p.208
9. Johnson and Boswell, *Journey to the Western Islands of Scotland*, Oxford 1930 p.72
10. *OSA*, vol.X p.354
11. Fraser Darling, Frank, *Crofting Agriculture*, London 1945, p.59
12. Martin, Martin, *A Description of the Western Isles of Scotland circa 1695*, Edinburgh 1984 pp. 243,
13. Dwelly, E., *The Illustrated Gaelic-English Dictionary,* Glasgow 1977
14. *The Scots Magazine* April, 1988, p.23
15. Stout, Margaret B., *The Shetland Cookery Book*, Lerwick 1965 pp.58,59
16. Mitchell, Arthur, *The Past in the Present*, Edinburgh 1980 p.45
17. *Ibid.*, pp.46,47
18. *Tocher*, 14, p.221
19. Duncan, A., ed. *Hebridean Island Memories of Scarp*, Edinburgh 1995 p.137
20. Cameron, Archie, *Bare Feet and Tackety Boots*, Luath Press p.57
21. Mackenzie, W. Leslie, *Scottish Mothers and Children*, The Carnegie United Kingdom Trust, Dunfermline 1917 p.447
22. Cameron, A. D., *Go Listen to the Crofters*, Acair 1986 p.21
23. *Ibid.*, p.81
24. *Report to the Secretary for Scotland by the Crofters Commission on the Social Conditions of the People of Lewis in 1901 as compared with 20 years ago.* p.xcvii
25. Shaw, Frances J., *The Northern and Western Islands of Scotland*, Edinburgh 1980 p.66
26. Cameron, A. D., *Go Listen to the Crofters*, Acair 1986 p.40
27. Walker, Dr. John, ed. Mackay, M.M., *Report on the Hebrides of 1764 and 1771*, Edinburgh 1980 p.65

28. Seton, George, *St. Kilda,* Edinburgh 1980 p.135
29. Nicolson, A., ed. *Gaelic Proverbs*, Edinburgh 1996 p.294
30. Bishop Forbes, *The Lyon in Mourning*, Edinburgh 1895, 3 vols., vol. 1, p.171
31. Nicolson, James R. *Traditional Life in Shetland*, London 1990 p.80
32. Stout, Margaret B.,*The Shetland Cookery Book*, Lerwick, 1965 p.59
33. *Ibid.*, p.59
34. Macdonald, Donald, Lewis Shielings, *Review of Scottish Culture*, no.1, 1984
35. Martin, Martin *A Description of the Western Isles of Scotland circa 1695*, Edinburgh 1984 p.457
36. Pennant, Thomas, *A Tour in Scotland and Voyage to the Hebrides, 1772,* Edinburgh 1998 p.204
37. Bishop Forbes, *The Lyon in Mourning*, Edinburgh 1895, 3 vols., vol.1, p.339
38. *Ibid.*, p.340
39. Grant, I. F., *Highland Folk Ways*, London 1961 p.126

Herring gutted and drying off. Dòmhnall, Ceiteag and Michaelina are keeping the flies away. Kilbride, South Uist, 1977.

Chapter 5: Fish

"Fish in fair weather they need not want; but, I believe, man never lives long on fish, but by constraint; he will rather live upon roots and berries."

Johnson and Boswell, *Journey to the Western Islands of Scotland*, Oxford 1930 p.92

Dh'iarr am muir a thadhal`

The sea wants to be visited - old Hebridean proverb

When Samuel Johnson visited the ruined Abbey of Iona in 1775 the fishponds were 'yet discernable' and the aqueduct which had supplied them was still in use.[1] The monks had wisely arranged, through this early fish farming, a regular supply of food. In the islands freshwater fish were plentiful, though increasingly a more commercial breed of landowners and their factors guarded their rights in this area extremely closely. During a walk across the machair of South Uist F.G. Rea and a companion came across a stream,

> about six or seven feet in width and running in a clean-cut channel ... At first I did not see what he was gazing at; then I became aware that hundreds and hundreds of trout were rushing inland up the stream; they were so closely packed that the water seemed scarcely sufficient to contain them ... this stream was an effluent of the Howmore river and these waters were strictly watched and preserved for the sport of the proprietor and his friends ...[2]

Such streams could, however, be blocked in several places with huge bundles of heather known as *caimhleacadh* where the trout would be trapped over night and quietly pulled out in the morning.[3] Interestingly, in Lewis, trout was not considered much of a meal.[4] Until the arrival of the Seaforths, salmon were caught in the Grimersta, Barvas, Laxay, Creed, Laxdale and Gress rivers with rods or traps.[5] Enough of the poacher`s equipment has survived to indicate that salmon was a common dish.[6]

Sea fish were for anyone's taking; poignant therefore, was the plight of the people of Canna which Pennant discovered in 1772. In spite of numerous cattle and good grazing [7]

> they were at this very time in such want, that numbers for a long time had neither bread nor meal for their poor babes: fish and milk was their whole subsistence at this time: the first was a

> precarious relief, for, besides the uncertainty of success, to add to their distress, their stock of fish-hooks was almost exhausted; and to ours, that it was not in our power to supply them. The ribbons, and other trifles I had brought would have been insults to people in distress. I lamented that my money had been so uselessly laid out; for a few dozens of fish-hooks, or a few pecks of meal, would have made them happy. [8]

Johnson too understood the precarious nature of fishing. While in Skye and on a visit to the caves of Ulinish he found a little boy,

> upon the point of a rock, catching with his angle, a supper for the family.

They persuaded him to lend them his rod, with which Boswell immediately caught a cuddy. Noting the abundance of fish, Johnson added, somewhat wistfully that,

> if it were always practicable to fish, these Islands could never be in much danger from famine, but unhappily, in the winter, when other provision fails, the seas are commonly too rough for nets, or boats. [9]

Fish were plentiful, but the sea conditions around such exposed coasts made it often quite impractical to take to boats for fishing. The naturalist Kearton, always an enthusiast, chose a calm day for his splendid afternoon's fishing (from a boat) accompanied by the Minister, during his stay on St. Kilda. [10] After an hour's trawling,

> I had seventeen Coalfish of an aggregate weight of something between one hundred and eighty and two hundred pounds.

Back on shore he left them to be shared among the inhabitants.

> When Sandy Campbell saw the boys dragging the fish past our cottage, he told me that he recollected the time when the St. Kildans would not eat it, as they said it had no substance (oil) in it. They simply took the liver out of such as they caught, and either cured the body for exportation or threw it to their dogs.[11]

For the Hebrideans, fish was not a food of choice. Some shellfish were eaten; whelks and winkles, which cling to the rocks closest to the sea were boiled and picked out with a pin[12] but limpets were a famine food, although not for the people of Swona, off Caithness.

> The inhabitants of the rest of the Orcades despise those of Swona for eating limpets, as being the last of human meannesses.[13]

During late June in the Bay of Meil Pennant records how,

> A boat filled with women and children crosses over from Jura, to collect their daily wretched fare, limpets and periwinkles.[14]

The combing of beaches for morsels was the lot of those perennially in want. The minister of Durinish recorded in the New Statistical Account how,

> shellfish is very abundant whenever the beach is smooth, and is much prized by the poorest of the people, to many of whom it affords sustenance in the latter end of summer, when generally every other provision fails.[15]

Most fish for domestic consumption were caught from the rocks or the shore by simple methods. *Corraig* in Gaelic indicates not just a rock but a good fishing rock. On the west side of South Uist flounders could be speared with a *brod-liabag*, a thin pointed stick with a ring about two inches from the foot.[16] When Prince Charles Edward Stuart landed in Eriskay,

> they catched some flounders, which they roasted upon the bare coals in a mean low hut.[17]

All the year round islanders caught inshore fish on small lines - flounders, sole, skate, haddock, gurnards and dogfish. Each one consisted of four strings of about twenty-one fathoms long with horsehair *davins*, each baited into a tiny basket made of wood or willow to stop them tangling.[18] Young coalfish known as saithe or sillocks were a staple food, said by the 'improvers' to be of particular nutritional value.

> The poor people observe, that when they live upon any other fish, without bread, which is often the case, they are never sufficiently nourished, but a weakness of their whole body ensues, but when they feed upon seath, whither with bread or not, it proves equally healthfull and nourishing.[19]

This could be construed as wishful thinking on Walker`s part, as saithe was a common fish which conveniently bridged the hungry time before the meal harvest came in. In Shetland, where crops were short such fish were dried, ground and used in place of meal. Archie Cameron on Rum reckoned that fishing for

> saithe was a lengthy, painful and sometimes unrewarding occupation. If the shoals were on the reefs, we had a good haul, and frequently enjoyed a potful of them boiled when we got them home, any hour after midnight.[20]

Saithe could be taken with rods or a large spoon-net called a *tabh* which was made with a big hoop of osier and two ribs in the middle crossing over each other.

> And on top of these ribs was a net, fixed round the rim of it. A great long handle, roughly ten feet. And they would go to the craigs with the tabh. The first thing they had to do was go and gather *soll*. Well, soll is what they called limpets, whelks,

> limpets and little things like that pounded up together. When they had pounded that up they would call it ground-bait. They would let down the tabh into the sea: they would scatter the ground-bait over it, and the cuddies would come to the bait. When they saw there was enough round the bait, they would raise the tabh and the poor little cuddies were in the middle of it.[21]

After cleaning, the fish were soaked in a heavy brine, (one that would float a potato) and hung up to dry.

> They are quite tasty ... if you boil them maybe three times, you know, put three waters on, bring to the boil three times, you take the salt out of them.[22]

Plenty of fish caught for home consumption was eaten fresh, but preservation was important for those hungry times when the dangerous sea lashed the coast and other foods were scarce. Drying was the simplest method, either outside on a frame attached to the house or in the *cleits* of the Hebrides and the *skeos* of the Northern Isles; little stone huts through which the the winds could blow. This *blawen* or *gozened* fish was pungent and strong tasting; much liked by people whose daily food was bland. Dog fish, being oily, was particularly well suited to drying. Long after the skeos had fallen into disuse, *kiossed-heeds* - fish heads or small fish were rolled in a cloth and stored in a crevice of the house wall until they had turned.[23]

Dried fish required soaking and careful cooking. Ned Bourk, when camping with Prince Charles Edward Stewart on Island Euirn did not relish the ones they found upon the rocks, left there by fishermen doubtless intending to return when the wind and sun had done their work. He

> began to complain that the fish would make but a very sarless morsel without butter.

Fortunately butter was produced, and all was well.[24] The same month they were in Benbecula where the boatman found a large crab or *partan* in the shallows and successfully fished for lyth.[25] As they had by then broken the earthen pitcher left by the fishermen[26] it is likely that they cooked their fish in hot ashes, perhaps wrapped in grass.

Smoking and salting were the other methods of preservation. Fish, with or without salting hung in the *reest* or rafters to dry and were soon lightly smoked.[27] Skate could not be first salted because of the impermeable mucus it exuded; in the roof it became *sour skate*, popular in spite of its strong smell of ammonia.[28] *Sookit whiting* was lightly salted and dried in the sun; ling, cod, tusk and saithe were all treated in the same way, gutted, washed in the sea and then packed with layers of salt which dissolved to a pickle. When weather conditions were right the fish were turned out on the beach to dry[29].

Sea fishing in small boats is surely one of the most dangerous activities known to man. It requires a supply of timber for good boats, expertise to build them and the skill and energy to sail them. It needs nets and lines which are arduous to make. Bait has to be found. If fishing is to be commercialized reliable methods of preservation, transport and markets are all necessary and not least, safe landing places for boats and men. In the late eighteenth century economic exploitation of the fishing gounds seemed an ideal way of 'improving' the condition of the islands. In 1786 John Knox, under the auspices of The British Fisheries Society, visited the north-west coast of Scotland in philanthropic mood and persuaded them, on his return, to provide funds for the building of a scattering of fishing villages such as Oban, Tobermory and Ullapool. The decline of the kelp industry and a rising, hungry population was turning many crofters to fishing out of necessity where they had been settled on more marginal, coastal land. Some landowners, middlemen and the Society itself provided boats and tackle. In Mull the Duke of Argyll

> divided a farm in Ross, convenient for the white fishing into a number of crofts. Here his Grace settled some families of country people; and to instruct them in curing the fish properly, he brought ... some fishers from Shetland ... which he settled among them. He gave them all the most liberal terms: he distributed the crofts among them at a low rent; provided them with boats and lines gratis, built a storehouse for their fish, and grinded meal for their use. In short, he provided them with every necessary,

> that their attention might be solely taken up with the fishing. But still the fishing by no means answered the expectations that might be reasonably entertained of its success.[30]

Yet in spite of a widespread lack of expertise, local subsistence fishing did eventually swell into a more organised industry with curing stations off the east coast of Barra and Lewis. In Shetland almost every activity was in some way connected with the sea. The eighteenth century merchant lairds acted as middlemen for the crofter-fishermen. They saw to the importing of salt, lines, hooks and other equipment. After 1750 coastal fish stocks of cod and ling became less certain and fish had to be found in deeper and more dangerous waters. By the beginning of the nineteenth century, for the purposes of deep-sea or *haaf* fishing a six-oared boat had replaced the three man yole. In a first-hand account of the 1881 gale,

> ... one man from North Roe ... who held on to his lines ... he rode out the gale out at sea, which perhaps wasn't a bad idea because in the very deep water the sea didn't break and the Shetland sixareen was a very, very buoyant, safe boat, so long as she didn't come into breakin water: it was what the old men called the land watter, where the sea was breakin on the boddom and on the rocks, most of the damage was done.[31]

By the time of the Napier Commission sixerns were being replaced by bigger and even safer boats, sometimes provided by the curers who bought all the fish at set prices agreed at the start of the season.

Along the Unst coastline stand the remains of stone lodgings and a fishing station where the men lived between the end of May and the middle of August, while the women kept the crofts. Throughout the islands there were customs and traditions connected with the food fishermen took to sea. Pork and ham were particularly unlucky. In Tiree,

> they didn't like to bring cheese or meat with you to sea, cheese or meat or eggs. Eggs was out of the question. They were scared of eggs. If they ... knew that you took eggs for your breakfast they

> wouldn't allow you on the boat to go with them. There is not a thing in the world that will carry so much evil as an egg ... an ordinary hen's egg ...[32]

The same belief is recorded in Barra, where

> there were others of them who thought that if they saw a rabbit they wouldn`t get any fish either.[33]

An old Ness fisherman believed the tastiest food he ever ate was the liver of a young dogfish mixed with oatmeal.

> This he placed under him on the thwart of a boat as he rowed to the fishing grounds. After an hour's rowing it tasted delicious![34]

In Orkney herring fishing and salting expanded dramatically during the nineteenth century. In the Hebrides the herring shoals that wintered in the sea lochs and appeared in summer off-shore in vast numbers[35] had always been an important food supply and a source of bait. The herring were gutted by the women and laid neatly and tightly in a large wooden barrel by one of the men, each layer being covered with coarse salt. When the salt had dissolved into a brine the fish was relaid with less salt in a clean barrel for winter use.[36] With the establishment of curing stations fish provided not just food but work, from Yarmouth to Stornoway.

There the cod, ling, torsk and saithe were processed, but the skate, halibut, turbot, flounder, crab, or other edible sea creature were the fishermens' own - to take back to his family.[37] Apart from these perquisites, it was customary all over for the fishermen to get the heads and livers, they therefore play an important part in the culinary tradition of the islands. Donald Moar of North Yell explained how they

> just give the fish to the curer. We have nothing to do but take off the heads. We get the heads and liver and keep them for our own purposes.[38]

Marion McNeill attributes cod-liver bannocks to Barra,[39] but various mixtures of liver and meal were universal simply because the amount of available fish liver exceeded the amount of fish. This is illustrated by a glance over the number of recipes in which fish liver was used, as in this recipe from a traditional Shetland Cookery Book.[40]

Liver Krolls
Four handfuls of Beremeal
Pinch of Salt
Cold water to mix
Small cup of Sillock Livers

Mix the meal to a paste with water; form into a round cake with hollow in the centre. Fill with liver and seasoning; cook either in oven or on brand-iron.
A similar bannock was made with burstin. Fresh livers were also put between dried fish for baking and added to cooked, flaked flesh, from the heads. This was known as *stapp*.

Similarly in Lewis,

> "cod and ling were gutted before they were given to the curers, and the heads, livers, and the three-quarter section of back-bone extracted, were regarded as the fisherman's."[41]

From these ingredients were made *Ceann Cropaig* and *Stuffed Gullet*, which are worth quoting in full.

> Cream the livers used, e.g. from haddock, cod, ling, or coalfish. After all the blood vessels have been removed, oatmeal, pepper and salt are added. The mixture has to be soft for if too much oatmeal were used the *ceann cropaig* would be hard. Fill the heads of fish with the mixture after the heads have been thoroughly cleaned. Boil for 20 minutes. For stuffed gullet it was preferable

> to use ling liver in a cod gullet if this were at all possible as the ling liver was richer and more nourishing than a cod`s, whereas the cod's gullet was stronger than a ling's and so less liable to burst. Gullet was about a third filled with pieces of livers, a little water and seasoning added and then boiled for 10-15 minutes.[42]

> Stuffed cods' heads was a fairly common dish, and there was always keen rivalry for the eyeballs after the head had been boiled,

remembered Archie Cameron.

> They resembled small white marbles, and flaked off gradually in the mouth. With careful sucking and manipulation, an eyeball would last all day.[43]

In Shetland, to make *krappit heeds*, or stuffed fish heads housewives used chopped livers, well seasoned with salt and pepper, mixed with oatmeal. The *muggie* or stomach could be cleaned and filled similarly with meal and livers, or with livers alone. Saithe were boiled with their liver until the oil floated on the water. This *gree* was skimmed off and poured over the fish.

> Slott was fish-roe beat with a spoon till it was like cream, a little flour with salt added, and the slott, roughly shaped into balls, was dropped into boiling water and boiled a short time. When cooled it was sliced, fried in butter, and eaten hot.[44]

This was a nutritious, if monotonous diet. Shetlanders reporting to the Napier Commission recognised the benefits of the herring boom, but were equally aware that catches of cod and ling were down in winter. Fish and the proceeds from it alone were not enough to feed their families.

> The fisherman needs a croft to fall back on, its harvest to sustain him, and his home to shelter him. Potatoes and fish are the staple food of Shetland,

reported John Spence, the teacher at Nesting.[45]

Fish fed the islanders and commercial fishing provided an opportunity to earn money. But it did not provide security. No-one could live by the produce of the cruel sea alone. In the Northern Isles a stronger tradition existed, but in the Hebrides the situation was palpably different.

> Indeed, the people there, taken as a whole, do not pretend to have any acquaintance with, or love for, a sea-faring life ... A few years ago a local priest made a collection of hymns, consisting of some old Gaelic hymns, translations from the Latin ... The Husbandman's Hymn, Laoidh an Tuathanaich, which forms one of the collection, is the production of a local bard, and a very creditable production it is. He, however, declined to compose a similar hymn applicable to the fishing, on the ground that he had no acquaintance with the fisherman's methods. A Fisherman's Hymn, Laoidh an Iasgair, was however, duly produced, but it is the composition of a mainlander.[46]

References — chapter 5

1. Boswell and Johnson, *Journey to the Western Islands of Scotland*, Oxford 1930 p.137
2. Rea, F. G., *A School in South Uist*, London 1864 pp.196,197
3. *Tocher*, 20 p.157
4. Macdonald, Donald, *Lewis A History of the Island*, Edinburgh 1978 p.55
5. *Ibid.*, p.56
6. Grant, I. F., *Highland Folk Ways*, London 1961 pp.342,343
7. Pennant, Thomas, *A Tour in Scotland and Voyage to the Hebrides, 1772*, Edinburgh 1998 p.270
8. *Ibid.*, p.271
9. Boswell and Johnson, *Journey to the Western Islands of Scotland*, Oxford 1930 p.6
10. Kearton, R., *With Nature and a Camera*, London 1904 p.67
11. *Ibid.*, p.69,70
12. *Annlan is Eile*, The Nicolson Institute, Stornoway, Lewis, 1978
13. Scott, Sir Walter, *The Voyage of the Pharos*, Edinburgh 1998 p.51
14. Pennant, Thomas, *A Tour in Scotland and Voyage to the Hebrides, 1772*, Edinburgh 1998 p.201
15. *NSA*, Vol.14 p.328
16. *Tocher* 20, p.159
17. Bishop Forbes, *The Lyon in Mourning*, Edinburgh 1895, 3 vols., vol.1, p.205
18. Macdonald, Donald, *Lewis A History of the Island*, Edinburgh 1978 p.93
19. Walker, Dr. John, ed. M. M. McKay, *Report on the Hebrides of 1764 and 1771*, Edinburgh 1980 p.49
20. Cameron, Archie, *Bare Feet and Tackety Boots*, Luath Press 1988 p.74
21. *Tocher* 20 p.159
22. *Tocher* 32 p.140
23. Saxby, M. R., *Shetland Traditional Lore*, Edinburgh 1932 pp.170,171
24. Bishop Forbes, *The Lyon in Mourning*, Edinburgh 1895, 3 vols., vol.1 p.171
25. *Ibid.*, pp.173,174
26. *Ibid.*, p.169
27. Walker, Bruce, Scottish Methods of Preserving White Fish, in *Gold Under the Furze, Studies in Folk Tradition*, ed. Gailey, Alan, and O'hOgain, Daithi, Dublin p.139
28. Nicolson, James R., *Traditional Life in Shetland*, London 1990 pp. 82,83
29. Walker, Bruce, Scottish Methods of Preserving White Fish, in *Gold Under the Furze, Studies in Folk Tradition*, ed. Gailey, Alan, and O'hOgain, Daithi, Dublin p.14
30. *OSA* vol. X1V p.287

31. *Tocher* 21, p.198
32. *Tocher* 20, p.152
33. *Tocher* 20, p.153
34. *Tocher* 11, p.119
35. The properties of the Fairy Flag at Dunvegan were threefold, produced in battle, it increased the numbers of Macleods, spread on the nuptial bed, it ensured fertility, last but not least, it brought herring into the loch.
Scott, Walter, *The Voyage of the Pharos*, Scottish Library Association 1998 p.81
36. Duncan, A., ed. *Hebridean Island Memories of Scarp*, Edinburgh 1995 p.24
37. Saxby, M. R., *Shetland Traditional Lore*, Edinburgh 1932 p.170
38. Cameron, A. D., *Go Listen to the Crofters*, Acair 1986 p.37
39. McNeill, Marion F., *The Scots Kitchen*, London 1930 p.109
40. Stout, Margaret B., *The Shetland Cookery Book*, Lerwick 1965 p.8
41. Macdonald, Donald, *Lewis A History of the Island*, Edinburgh 1978 p.95
42. *Tocher* 9 p.136
43. Cameron, Archie, *Bare Feet and Tackety Boots*, Luath Press 1988 p.50
44. Saxby, M. R., *Shetland Traditional Lore*, Edinburgh 1932 p.171
45. Cameron, A.D. *Go Listen to the Crofters*, Acair 1986 p.39
46. *Report to the Secretary of State for Scotland by the Crofters Commission, on the Social Conditions of the people of Lewis in 1901,* Glasgow 1902 p.LX 111

Taking off sheep for the pot, Boreray, Sound of Harris, 1979.

Chapter 6: Meat

Clanranald is my great treasure,
I knew the custom of your household,
Boiling beef and flaying cattle,

Campbell, J. L., ed. *Hebridean Folksongs*, Oxford 1981 3 vols., vol.3 p.231

Beef or mutton was very seldom used by the people; the animals producing the meat were kept till the annual market, and then sold to dealers who took them to the mainland of Scotland.

Rea, F.G., *A School in South Uist,* London 1964 p.153

November 1908, Thurs 9th. When we came home Angus G. came down with a piece of ancient mutton (killed a week and hanging in smoke since). It was awful.

Alice MacLachlan, St Kilda, 1906-1909 Quine, David A. *St Kilda Portraits,* p.101

In the islands animal husbandry was easy, compared with the struggle to raise crops.

> "The snow seldom lies deep or long; a circumstance highly favourable to sheep and black cattle.[1]

So wrote the minister of Barvas, Lewis, for the Old Statistical Account. The fact that fresh meat was hardly being consumed at all, reflects a situation where cattle had become almost entirely a cash crop. By the end of the eighteenth century it was customary for a farmer to sell about one fifth of his total stock, for rent, increasing amounts of meal, farm implements and salt. The majority of cattle went south on the drove roads, though about one quarter went salted to Glasgow.

> For want of a cask,

reported John Walker,

> they have a very singular method of salting and packing them up in hides, which preserves them very well ...[2]

Within the Hebrides St Kildans were an exception in the amount of meat they consumed. It was noted by Martin that,

> ... all their beef and mutton is eaten fresh.[3]

Their seabirds were simply wind-dried in the cleits, the people preferring to rely on that rich food source of preserved food and winter their beasts as well as they could. By spring, however, animals were in poor condition, unsuitable even for a funeral feast.

> ... they kill a cow, or sheep, before the interment, but if it be in the spring, this ceremony then is delayed, because the cattel are at that time poor and lean, but, however, they are to be kill'd as soon as ever they become fat.[4]

The new root and fodder crops that fed stock in winter came late to the Hebrides where it was hard for animals to survive the winter. Milch cows took precedence and were housed.

> The rest of the stock roamed outside, surviving as best they could on the scant herbage or the seaweed that was available at ebb-tide.[5]

Fresh meat was a rarity.[6] Most meat was preserved and only consumed on special occasions. In Shetland air-dried meat, or *vivda* gradually gave way to the salted and smoked. For the housewife this was an important task, so it is worth quoting these instructions in full.

SALTING OF BEEF

An average sized Shetland cow gives from 2-2 1/4 cwts. of beef, and 35-50 lb. of fat. Allow 10lbs salt to 1cwt of beef or roughly 1 bushel to 1 cow.

Method

Rub all the pieces of meat with salt and lay in a tub over night; this draws out the extra blood which might make the pickle impure. Next day, lift each piece out, allow to drip, rub with salt and lay each piece out separately. Weigh the remainder of salt and weigh out an equal quantity of brown sugar. Pack the barrel with meat, putting a

> layer of salt and sugar between each until full; put on lid which must have holes in it to allow of ventilation and set aside until salt becomes a brine. If this does not rise to the level of the top of the meat, make some extra pickle salt enough to float a potato, and pour this on. Meat pickled in this way will keep 6-9 months. If pickle show signs of decaying add fresh salt or turn out meat, wash, return to barrel with a little fresh salt strewn between each layer.
>
> *Note*.- A specially strong tight barrel is required for salting. In many country districts it is possible to buy a tiss or barrel which has been brought from the south with beef.[7]

The "boyled beef and pottage" produced for Prince Charles Edward Stewart in Skye had probably been preserved in a similar fashion, although without sugar.[8] Salted meat was removed from the barrel and thoroughly soaked in fresh water before cooking with grain, usually barley, and any available vegetables and herbs. The meat was then taken out of the pot and served cold - this, as all cooks know was more economical. The remaining liquid was then thickened with more meal to make a broth or soup, to be eaten with bread.

Another recipe from Shetland for preserving prime cuts advises firstly rubbing the meat over thoroughly with salt before making a pickle of more salt and water strong enough to float a potato in. The meat was first slit open and stuffed with a handful of salt and seasonings such as pepper, cayenne, cinnamon and nutmeg, then tied up, soaked in the pickle for 24 hours and hung up in the open air to dry. This was a light salting and would not last 6 to 9 months like the meat packed into barrels with layers of dry salt and brown sugar.[9] In fact Shetlanders preferred their meat *reested*, that is, smoked and dried rather than salted.[10] *Is fheàrr cuid na ciad oidhche na na h-oidhche mu dheireadh* - the first night's fare is better than the last night's[11] - is a guarded comment on winter beef in the Hebrides. Salted and dried venison from Kinloch lodge was the mainstay of winter meals on Rum.

> Some of that dried venison was really hard tack ... Choosing a suitable chunk, my mother would throw it on the concrete floor of the scullery, and lay into it with a hatchet.[12]

When reduced to manageable portions it was soaked all night and then put to cook with turnips. While in the Hebrides Samuel Johnson had noted that,

> they seldom taste the flesh of land animals; for here are no markets. What each man eats is from his own stock. The great effect of money is to break property into small parts. In towns, he that has a shilling may have a piece of meat; but where there is no commerce, no man can eat mutton but by killing a sheep.[13]

This problem was solved in part by the practice of buying a joint mart, whereby neighbours or households cooperated in buying a cow, sheep or even a goat for salting and sharing. (Goats were kept in the mountainous areas of Lewis, Park, Lochs and Uig.[14]) This institution may have given rise to the Gaelic proverb - *làn beòil de bhiadh, is làn baile de nàire* - a mouthful of meat, and a townful of shame[15]: the inference being that if a person seemed unaccountably to be in possession of a little meat, they had probably procured it illegally or immorally.

In the Northern Isles grazing was richer but the problem of winter feeding was the same. Around Martinmas (11 November) *mert* or mart beasts were slaughtered and salted down for winter eating. Mrs Jessie Saxby, in her book on *Shetland Traditional Lore* described how 'the breakin doon o da mert' was a most important event, and everybody lent a hand. No morsel of that cow was considered unfit for food, and every morsel of the creature had a name of its own descriptive of its functions when alive.'[16]

There was another source of meat, considered dubious by the less hungry. *Braxy* mutton was the salted flesh of a sheep which had died of braxy. Norman Macleod speaks of it as a species of mutton which need not be too minutely inquired into.[17] Braxy is in fact a bacterial infection of sheep which tended, ironically, to affect the fittest and fattest.

> But it did not affect the flesh ... (so) ... to find a newly dead braxy sheep was a find indeed, and a great help to the diet of the lucky family."[18] "On at least one occasion, (in Rum) we did not even have to look for the braxy sheep on the hill. The 'hoggs' or young ewes were usually sent to winter on the mainland, as the island winter

> was considered too extreme for them. On one of those trips two of the beasts died of braxy. They were in prime condition, and so were promptly given the last rites, which consisted of skinning and dressing. A rope was then smartly attached, and they were towed behind the Kinloch all the way to Kyle, where they were taken on board, liberally salted, and taken back to Rum, to provide more than a few good dinners. Certainly, well pickled and salted, braxy mutton was a grand change from the usual diet of salt saithe.[19]

Unlike the cattle, which were carefully tended, though they too succumbed to accidents and disease, the sheep and goats which grazed alongside them received little attention except when being milked or gathered for clipping or pulling of wool. Of course there were exceptions. Consider the St. Kildan who had himself and a favoured sheep lowered onto a grass-covered ledge far down the face of an 'awesome cliff' which

> he left to browse on the few mouthfuls of luscious grass for three or four days. That any sane being should risk so much for so little seemed to me incredible.[20]

No doubt they met with frequent accidents,[21] and were either salted, where salt was available, wind dried or quickly consumed. And it was not unknown for sheep to be 'helped' over a cliff in order to procure some fresh meat,[22] such a rare commodity that when a crofter from Achmore, Lewis, during February of 1851 was found to have some in his house, he was immediately apprehended by the sheriff's officers.

> McLeod when asked by the officers to account how he got the fresh meat told them it was a deer he had killed on the hill, when asked for the skin he replied that he was not in the habit of taking home the skin. This was all said to blind the officers as it was evidently stolen mutton.[23]

(The incident reflects a tacit tolerance of single-handed poaching.[24])

Every bit of sheep, cow or goat carcase was used. The sheep's head rejected by Johnson was a standard dish.[25] Intestines and offal, in particular, were of great value. In the Northern Isles from earliest times a small, native breed of pig was widespread and hams were being exported in considerable numbers. Some pigs roamed wild on the hill with all the attendant dangers.

> A clergyman ... walking in the fields ... heard the squeaking of a pig for some time, without being able to discern whence it proceeded, until looking up, he beheld the unfortunate grunter in the talons of an eagel, who soared away with him towards the summit of Hoy.[26]

Some were housed in special styes[27] and some shared a roof with their owners. In Fair Isle the practice appeared squalid to visitors but it showed the relative prosperity of the people. "I cannot wonder that they want meal," wrote Scott.

> A great bowie or wooden vessel of porridge is made in the morning; a child comes and sups a few spoonfuls; then Mrs Sow takes her share; then the rest of the children or the parents, and all at pleasure; then come the poultry when the mess is more cool; the rest is flung upon the dunghill – and the goodwife wonders and complains when she wants meal in winter.[28]

Pigs were rare in the Hebrides. A range of explanations are given; including the existence of an ancient and superstitious prejudice and the teaching of evangelical clergy. The most likely reason is simply that the people did not have the necessary food scraps to keep pigs, just as there was little poultry because grain was scarce. Pennant concluded that in Skye,

> Hogs are not introduced here yet, for want of proper food for those animals.[29]

By the 1840s improved breeds had usurped the native variety. Generally speaking, pigs were overwintered once and then killed in November. The kidneys were eaten immediately, their fat rendered down and any not put to immediate use stored in jars. The liver was much less palatable, being dry and rather hard. It had to be boiled, peeled and then fried in fat.[30] The heart was salted and used for soup. The lungs or *lights* might also be salted, along with the pork, but they were sometimes eaten fresh.

> However, the lungs had an ill reputation for disease, so in order to let any possible defects boil out, an inch or so of the windpipe was kept above water, tied with a string to the lid. It was thought that any bad germs would be forced out through this opening.[31]

There was a similar fear related to sheeps' lungs. In Lewis, after sheep slaughtering,

> It was a common sight to see the trachea hanging over the lip of the cooking pot with froth dribbling out of it.[32]

Pigs' brains could be fried with a lite oatmeal and the trotters, scalded and salted, being gelatinous, made good soup.

'Puddings' were an important and economical bye-product of all butchering. In Rum, during the early part of this century, if a sheep were killed the person arriving first at the slaughterhouse, with a bucket, received all the animal's internal tubes.[33] In Orkney the newly killed pigs' intestines were immediately cleaned. One end was tied off and the other end blown into and also tied. These 'blown puddings' were hung up to dry and later filled with a variety of ingredients including fat, oatmeal, flour and cabbage. When available currants, raisins and sugar were all used. Black puddings incorporated the blood of the slaughtered animal, echoing the older practice of bleeding live cattle and spreading the dried blood on bannocks. During pudding making clotting was prevented by adding salt to the pigs' blood.

There was a knack in not over-filling the intestines, but the puddings still had to be watched as they boiled over the fire and quickly pricked if they showed signs of splitting. A more luxurious sausage or *sparl* was made with chopped pork. This was boiled and eaten cold. Collops were cut fresh from the joints and fried. If there was plenty of pork fat left over in the pan, oatmeal and spice were stirred into it to make a rich dish called *hoonska*. The choicest pieces of meat were smoked and known as *reested pork*.

"When a cow was killed certain parts were laid aside for salting, drying and pickling." [34] Less choice scraps, fat and gristle off the breast and foreshoulder were chopped, well seasoned and put into the the largest sparls, with the fat left on. These were then laid in salt which melted into a brine. This was then thoroughly dried and the sausages hung up in the roof, where they would keep several months. The cow's udder could be roasted or boiled.

On Scarp Angus Duncan remembered being thrown the sheep's breast strip and tail strip by the butcher. The boys plucked the wool, singed it in the fire and then cooked it in the cinders until it was curled and ready for chewing. It was the butcher who turned the long intestine inside out and stuffed it with the chopped kidneys and liver and some suet. Then oatmeal was mixed with some congealed blood and added in. The pudding was immediately ready for cooking. The other entrails were cleaned out the next day and filled with various combinations of oatmeal, blood and offal. [35] The making of haggis involves stuffing the stomach with oatmeal, chopped heart and liver.

With meat a rarity, whales were highly prized, for they made good eating. [36] "There are many whales of different sizes, that frequent the herring bays on the east side," observed Martin Martin.

> The natives employ many boats together in pursuit of the whales, chasing them up into the bays, till they wound one of them mortally, and then it runs ashore; and they say that all the rest commonly follow the track of its blood, and run themselves also on shore in like manner by which many of them are killed. About five years ago there were fifty young whales killed in this manner, and most of them eaten by the common people, who by experience find them to be very nourishing food. This I have been assured of by several persons, but particularly by some poor meagre people, who became plump and lusty by this food in the space of a week: they call it seapork, for so it signifies in their language. The bigger whales are more purgative than these lesser ones, but the latter are better for nourishment. [37]

Whale could be smoked and made acceptable hams. In the Hebrides whale meat was definitely a poor man's food; in Shetland and Orkney, a famine food. There the whale oil was much prized,[38] and a Shetlander who had worked on the whaling ships which went to Greenland remembered older men heating chopped blubber in a tin and eating it.[39] *The Pharos*, towards the end of her journey (1814) passed

> a most curious spectacle, being no less than the carcases of two hundred and sixty-five whales, which have been driven ashore in Taftsness bay. In fact, this species of spectacle has been of late years very common among the isles. Mr. Stevenson saw upwards of a hundred and fifty whales lying upon the shore in a bay at Unst, in his northward trip. They are not large, but are decided whales, measuring perhaps from fifteen to twenty-five feet. They are easily mastered ...[40]

As in Martin's time, one wounded whale would draw the others to the shore where they could be killed in shallow water by means of a cut under the back fin with a long whaling knife. The sea would quickly resemble port wine.

Seals too were killed for meat but their slipperiness and agility made them a difficult prey and may have given rise to the belief that they could actually change their shape. Many old stories are based on this theme; the girl bride for example who hides her sealskin from her husband but eventually leaves him to return to the sea. Or the man cutting limpets for bait who comes upon a big seal which he then attempts to kill with just the limpet pick - an object like a broken knife with a wooden handle. He plunges the tool into the seal who struggles and makes off over the rocks, leaving him empty-handed. Years later an old lady returns him that same pick – the inference being that she and the seal are one and the same person.[41] Such was the value of seal fat at the end of the nineteenth century special expeditions were still made to the Heisgeir rocks in October to kill them for both oil and meat.[42]

A strong view persisted into the nineteenth century that in former times a larger population had lived more comfortably - from dairy products in summer and meat in winter.[43]

> In those primitive times, the forests, heaths, and waters, abounding with game and fish, were alike free to all, and contributed greatly to the support of the inhabitants.[44]

A significant number of reporters to the Napier Commission point to the decline in the availability of 'animal food'.

> A doctor in Skye believed there were no better navvies than Skyemen and hinted that this might be in part due to their food when they were away working, because he added, "But then they're having their beef three times a day.[45]

Undoubtedly there was nostalgia for a more plenteous past when resident chieftains and landlords had feasted their tenantry. For Sir Alexander Macdonald's funeral on 23rd November 1746 the factor in Trotternish, Ranald McAlestor, laid out £2645 Scots on provisions for the mourners, including meat and drink at Portree for their return from Sleat. On this memorable occasion the revelry got out of hand and three men were killed.[46]

References — chapter 6

1. *OSA vol. X1X pp.266,267*
2. Walker, Dr. John, ed. M. M. McKay, *Report on the Hebrides of 1764 and 1771*, Edinburgh 1980 p.87
3. Martin, Martin, *A Description of the Western Isles of Scotland circa 1695*, Edinburgh 1984 p.456
4. *Ibid.*, p.456
5. Macdonald, Donald, *Lewis A History of the Island*, Edinburgh 1978 p.81
6. Fenton, Alexander, *Scottish Country Life*, Edinburgh 1976 p.170
7. Stout, Margaret B., *The Shetland Cookery Book*, Lerwick 1965 pp.22,23
8. Bishop Forbes, *The Lyon in Mourning*, Edinburgh 1895 3 vols., vol.1 p.308
9. Stout, Margaret, *The Shetland Cookery Book*, Lerwick 1965 p.24
10. Saxby, M. R., *Shetland Traditional Lore*, Edinburgh 1932 p.172
11. Nicolson A., ed. *Gaelic Proverbs*, Edinburgh 1996 p.273
12. Cameron, Archie, *Bare Feet and Tackety Boots*, Luath Press 1988 p.31
13. Johnson and Boswell, Journey to the Western Islands of Scotland, Oxford 1930 p.92
14. MacDonald, Donald, *Lewis A History of the Island*, Edinburgh 1978 p.87
15. Nicolson A., ed. *Gaelic Proverbs*, Edinburgh 1996 p.333
16. Saxby, M. R., *Shetland Traditional Lore*, Edinburgh 1932 p.172
17. McNeill, F. Marian, *The Scots Kitchen*, Edinburgh 1930 p.23
18. Cameron, Archie, *Bare Feet and Tackety Boots*, Luath Press 1988 p.73
19. *Ibid.*, pp.73,74
20. Kearton, R., *With Nature and a Camera*, London 1904 pp.41,42
21. *Ibid.*, p.87
22. Cameron, Archie, *Bare Feet and Tackety Boots*, Luath Press 1988 p.13
23. Mackenzie, John Munro, *Diary 1851*, Acair 1994 p.31
24. Grant, I.F. *Highland Folk Ways*, London 1961 p.342
25. Johnson and Boswell, *Journey to the Western Islands of Scotland*, Oxford 1930 p.391
26. Scott, Walter, *The Voyage of the Pharos*, Scottish Library Association 1998 p.59
27. An example of a stone-built pig stye can be seen at the Newtonmore Folk Park, Highland Folk Museum, Inverness-shire
28. Scott, Walter, *The Voyage of the Pharos*, Scottish Library Association 1998 p.38
29. Pennant, Thomas, *A Tour in Scotland and Voyage to the Hebrides, 1772*, Edinburgh 1998 p.311
30. Boiling and then frying was a common way of rendering less-appealing meat edible

31. Fenton, Alexander, *The Northern Isles: Orkney and Shetland,* Edinburgh 1978 p.503
32. Macdonald, Donald, *Lewis A History of the Island*, Edinburgh 1978 p.55
33. Cameron, Archie, *Bare Feet and Tackety Boots*, Luath Press 1988 p.78
34. Stout, Margaret B., *The Shetland Cookery Book,* Lerwick 1965 p.25
35. Duncan, A., ed. *Hebridean Island Memories of Scarp*, Edinburgh 1995 p.93
36. Muck, or the isle of pigs, may be connected with sea pork, i.e. whale-meat
37. Martin, Martin *A Description of the Western Isles of Scotland circa 1695*, Edinburgh 1984 p.88
38. Fenton, Alexander, *The Northern Isles: Orkney and Shetland,* Edinburgh 1978 p.545
39. *Tocher* 22, p.231
40. Scott, Walter, *The Voyage of the Pharos*, Scottish Library Association 1998 p.43
41. *Tocher* 34, p.274
42. Kearton, *With Nature and a Camera*, London 1904 p.3
43. Hunter, James, *The Making of the Crofting Community*, Edinburgh 1976 p.92
44. Stewart, Col. David, *Sketches of the Character, Manners and Present State of the Highlanders of Scotland*, Edinburgh 1822 2vols., vol.1 p.132
45. Cameron, A. D., *Go Listen to the Crofters*, Acair 1986 p.103
46. *Lord Macdonald`s Estate Papers*, Clan Donald Library, Armadale, Skye

Finlay MacQueen with rod to catch puffins, St. Kilda, 1896.

Chapter 7: Wildfowling

Suas mo lòn, nuas mo ruba
Chuala mis' an gug sa chuan

(Up my rope, up my snare,
I have heard the gannet on the sea)

Carmichael, Alexander, *Carmina Gadelica*, Edinburgh 1941 6 vols., vol.4 p.109

The annual harvest of seabirds and their eggs was arguably the most reliable food source in the islands in those places where nesting took place. Come wind, come weather, the birds would return to their nesting places and as long as the skills and the determination to hunt them remained in the communities the people could be assurred of a rich and reliable supply of protein and fat as well as oil and feathers for trade. Before the people could procure a good supply of salt, [1] the birds were air-dried for winter eating by the ceaseless wind in well-ventilated stone huts known in the Hebrides as *cleits* and in Orkney and Shetland as *skeos*, which were also used in the drying of meat and fish. In particular the people of St. Kilda and their survival was inextricably linked to their fowling economy. Visitors were without exception fascinated and amazed by the apparent risks and the extreme dangers endured by the men who climbed the highest cliffs in Britain in search of birds and their eggs.

> As the stranger walks along the path in front of the houses he is stuck by three things - the strong smell of fulmar oil, the plenitude of birds` wings and feathers on the midden heaps, and the number of birds eggs that adorn nearly every window. [2]

But there were other places, less known and less trumpeted by Victorian writers where seabirds were also an important food source. The men of Ness made and still make an annual expedition to Sula Sgeir, a rock forty miles off the coast of Lewis to catch the young gannets, or 'guga'. Foula in Shetland was particularly dependent on fowling, producing some of the most famously skilled climbers. A visitor in 1818 remembered a particularly dramatic coastal walk when,

> on reaching the highest of the rocks, the prospect presented on every side is of the sublimest description. The spectator looks down from a perpendicular height of 1100 or 1200 feet, and sees below the wide Atlantic roll its tide. Dense columns of birds hover through the air, consisting of maws, kittywakes, lyres, sea-parrots, or guillemots; the cormorants occupy the lowest portions of the cliffs, the kittywakes whiten the ledges of one distinct cliff, gulls are found on another, and lyres on a third. The welkin is darkened

> with their flight; nor is the sea less covered with them, as they search the waters in quest for food. ... From the brink of this awful precipice the adventurous fowler is, by means of a rope tied round his body, let down many fathoms; he then lands on the ledges, where the various sea birds nestle, being still as regardless as his ancestors of the destruction that awaits the falling of some loose stones from a crag or the untwisting of a cord. It was formerly said of the Foula man, "his gutcher (grandfather) guid before, his father guid before, and he must expect to go over the Snerry too.[3]

Fowling was important in Mingulay too, and in Barra where,

> they take great numbers of seafowls from the adjacent rocks, and salt them with the ashes of burnt sea-ware in cows' hides which preserves them from putrefaction ...[4]

It can reasonably be assumed that everywhere in the islands where they were to be found, seabirds and their eggs provided a good source of food. Cormorants and shags were taken the whole year round in the sea caves and headlands of Mull.[5] In Orkney guillemots' eggs were regularly gathered off the island of Copinsay up until the First World War,[6] and the boys of Rum were collecting the eggs of gulls and eider ducks into the twentieth century.

> Eider duck eggs were a highly rated bonus in our annual safari for seagull eggs, and were considered a great delicacy. There was never any doubt about what you had found when you came on an eider duck nest ... When the duck left the nest, frightened away without having had time to conceal the eggs from predators (and we were predators), she emptied her bowels as she took off, and the stink of that mess was enough to daunt all except the most hungry and hardy predators. We were of the first category. As a matter of fact, we were alerted by the smell.[7]

The eggs of the lapwing were also considered a delicacy.[8] Handa, the Shiants, North Rona, Sulasgeir, the Flannans, Mingulay, Berneray (Barra) Canna, the Treshnish Isles and Colonsay are all important nesting sites for the twenty two species of seabird which breed in the Hebrides, but one third of all those birds, and indeed, one tenth of all those breeding in Britain and Ireland do so at St. Kilda.[9]

The gannet or solan goose begins to arrive from its winter quarters in West Africa from the end of January. With its six-foot wing span, gliding flight and dramatic diving skills, it is a magnificent bird. Despite the fact that during the eighteenth century it is probable that the St. Kildans were taking at least 20,000 of these birds annually from Stac Lee and Stac an Armin alone, St. Kilda remains the world's biggest gannetry.

The most numerous species of sea birds are puffin, fulmar, Manx shearwater, guillemot, razorbill, kittiwake and gannet. More than 100,000 pairs of puffins breed at St. Kilda alone. Out of necessity the boys of St. Kilda learned to climb as they learned to walk. The distribution and range of sea-birds has probably remained fairly constant over the last millennium which gives Martin's account of the bird-men a timeless significance. Sea-bird fowling, even in Martin's time was the exception rather than the rule, even in remoter communities, which does something to explain the curiosity he showed in it and the vivid quality of his account. In Mingulay he described the scaling of Linmull, a rock

> indifferently high, and almost inaccessible, except in one place, and that is by climbing, which is very difficult. This rock abounds with sea-fowls that build and hatch here in summer; such as the guillemot, coulterneb, puffin, etc. The chief climber is commonly called Gingich, and this name imports a big man having strength and courage proportionable. When they approach the rock with the boat, Mr. Gingich jumps out first upon a stone on the rock-side and then by the assistance of a rope of horse-hair, he draws his fellows out of the boat upon this high rock, and draws the rest up after him with the rope, until they all arrive at the top, where they purchase a considerable quantity of fowls and eggs. Upon their return to the boat, this Gingich runs a great hazard by jumping first into the boat again, where the violent sea

> continually rages; having but a few fowls more than his fellows, besides a greater esteem to compensate his courage.[10]

The fowler with status and prestige is portrayed as hero, overcoming all dangers to reach the birds. On St Kilda young men brought birds to their sweethearts and were obliged to prove their climbing skills before marriage. Fowling was the key to providing. Many stories exist relating to the strength, daring, bravery and luck of the fowlers.

It was not easy to hunt the gannet. The birds did not nest on the main island of Hirta, so it was necessary to make a dangerous sea voyage across to Boreray. The "creeping fowlers" worked under cover of darkness, either climbing up the rock with their horse-hair and hide ropes attached around their waists or being lowered from above onto the ledges where the gannets slept. Martin describes how a sentinel bird

> cries softly, grog, grog, at which the flock move; but if this centinel see or hear the fowler approaching, it cries quickly, bir, bir, which would seem to import danger, since immediately after, all the tribe take wing, leaving the fowler empty on the rock ...[11]

Some birds were caught in horse hair traps, from which they did not make much attempt to escape. Unlike the fulmar, for example, the gannet would lay again if its egg were removed. So in the middle of May a first egg-collecting expedition took place, though Stac Lee was left, so that there the young gannet, or guga, would be ready to harvest earlier.

The St. Kildans ate eggs in huge numbers. Martin calculates that 16,000 were "bestowed upon those of our boat, and the Stewart's birlin ... "[12] Some were eaten fresh but it seems they were particularly liked when they had begun to turn. Their flavour was described as astringent.

> They preserve their eggs commonly in their stone-pyramids, scattering the burnt ashes of turf under and about them to defend them from the air, dryness being their only preservative, and moisture their corruption; they preserve them six, seven, or eight months, as above said; and then they become appetizing and loosening, especially those that begin to turn.[13]

Fowler with rod and catch of gannets, St. Kilda, 1896.

The loosening quality of bad eggs must have been extremely desirable. John Reid, an artist who visited Foula in 1867 and was given boiled eggs for breakfast, lunch and tea recommended a pocket enema to other travellers.[14]

Although Martin visited St. Kilda when the gannet harvest was at its height, he noted that for eating, the people preferred the fulmar,

> whether young or old ... the old is of a delicate taste, being a mixture of fat and lean; the flesh white, no blood is to be found but only in its head and neck; the young is all fat, excepting the bones, having no blood but what is in its head; and when the young fulmar is ready to take wing, it being approached, ejects a quantity of pure oyl out at its bill ... this oyl is sometimes of a reddish, sometimes of a yellow colour, and the inhabitants and other islanders put a great value upon it, and use it as a catholicon for diseases, especially for any aking in the bones ...[15]

From the 1750s the fulmar became the principal bird caught and eaten by the St. Kildans, but the gannet harvest continued, albeit on a smaller scale. Alice MacLachlan, who spent the years 1906 to 1909 on St. Kilda where her husband Peter was the Missionary, noted in her diary for Tuesday 9 April, 1907 that the men were off to Boreray after the Solan goose. The following day, Wednesday 10,

> Went down on the pier after breakfast to see the gannets killed last night. There were a good few over 100. Each who went had about 30 apiece. We got a pair. I am collecting the large quills. They are lovely for hats. [16]

Apart from taste, there were obvious reasons for this change; the fulmar nested on Hirta, stayed longer and provided not just good, white meat but oil and feathers for export. But even in this seemingly inconsequential development can be sensed the seeds of the decline of fowling as an elite activity with a sporting dimension; the trophies laid out for all to admire and distributed as token gifts to people of status.

August was the fulmar season.

> The people started killing the fulmar on Friday (Aug.16.) and have had very good weather so far. [17]

So wrote the missionary's wife on August 24, 1907. Before fowling started in earnest the ropes were tested and the cliff are shared out. In the eighteenth century horsehair and hide ropes were communally owned but by the nineteenth century individual families had their own. In the last fifty years of the island`s existence hemp ropes were universal, although there was still an old hair one for Kearton to buy and remove as a souvenir in 1895. [18]

John Ross, a school teacher in St. Kilda, 1889 wrote with a certain degree of hesitation about the culinary delights of seabirds.

> The fulmar, when young and fresh is best roasted. Indeed, when properly done this way and when one has the nerve to start, it tastes fairly well. Something like young pork, but as tender as chicken. [19]

The fishy flavour of seabirds is in the fat and the usual cooking method of boiling would reduce it, especially if the water was changed during cooking.[20] Cormorants and shags taken in the Uists and Harris were sometimes skinned rather than plucked which removed some of the outer layer of fat and with it some of the fishy flavour. Par-boiling and frying was a more luxurious cooking method for a variety of seabirds including auk, a dark meat not unlike beef and its offal and kittiwake, similar to chicken.[21] One Orkney cook describes preparing cormorant.

> The birds were skinned and hung up for a while. Some people, she said, wrapped a cloth round them and buried them in the earth for a week. They were then par-boiled in several waters, pouring the water away each time; the bones were all picked out and the flesh put in a stew pan with butter, plenty of onions and pepper, and in some cases a little minced pork or ham.[22]

Sir Walter Scott (1771-1832), having shot some cormorants in one of Loch Eribol's caves noted that,

> the Zetlanders made excellent hare-soup out of these sea-fowl.[23]

In St. Kilda, the majority of the fulmar harvest was plucked, drawn, split open and air-dried in the small, stone cleits scattered around the island. The fulmar oil which the bird will spit in self defence was carefully collected and stored in bags made of the stomachs of gannets. Some authorities suggest that each bird gives about half a pint of oil. The naturalist, Kearton thought this an over estimate, noting also how,

> the oil gives off such a strong odour that everything in St. Kilda smells of it ...[24]

Guillemot were the earliest arrivals of the year, captured during February[25] as they flew in at dawn to perch on the lower rocks. This first fresh food of the year was awaited with great anticipation.

> No sooner would the fowler drop his catch at the cottage door ... than willing hands would carry the birds to the byre where they would be split and cleaned and plucked. That day the big pot would swing above the peat flame. The fire would be frequently stirred ... Even the dogs would come, passing to and fro in an almost unending procession ... for the dogs of Hirt knew as well as its people the difference of a six months old fulmar just from the pickle barrel, and a plump fresh gilliemot or sheerwater fresh from the cliffs.[26]

Later their beautiful eggs made delicious eating. Kearton enjoyed them for breakfast on Ailsa Craig.[27] The fowlers captured guillemot by means of a human lure, whereby the hunter, disguised as a guano-covered rock, would wring their necks as they landed. This is graphically described by Christina MacQueen, a native of St. Kilda.

> Men who, in the darkness of an April night, and until dawn, crept up beyond the distant Harris hills, would be grouped upon the cliff tops, while far below, with a rope round his middle, one of their comrades would sit, his body swathed in a white sheet - a lure for the birds that come in the night.
>
> There he would sit, a thousand feet above the sea, waiting, watching, listening. Up above men would talk in whispers ... Just before dawn the first bird would come, wearied, no doubt, with its long flight over the sea (for most of the birds of Hirt go off at the fall ...) In from the sea it would fly, straight for the white spot that it fondly imagined marked the place of its last years lodgment; the place where it mated and nested and reared its young. Then would that fowler of Hirt have work to do. Quick and deft would he use his hands. There would be no time to lose. Death must come swiftly and silently to those first heralds of a Hirtach`s harvest. No sooner would its bright yellow webbed feet seek a landing place on the fowler`s head or in his lap, than it would be instantly despatched. Not a sound would the fowler

> make. Not a cheep from the bird. The others must not be warned of the trap that holds death in its coaxing whiteness. So the fowler sits and waits. The ledge at his side grows whiter with the still, warm bodies of the slain. As he waits he hears but the muffled booming of the surf a thousand feet below - the strange sea music that is Hiort's ...[28]

Puffin nested on St. Kilda in their thousands. Sometimes they were driven from their burrows by dogs, sometimes caught in snares and sometimes taken with a fowling rod. This was a highly skilled operation. The rods were made of deal, approximately thirteen feet long with about a yard of hazel twig lashed to the end to which is attached a running noose of horse hair stiffened with gannet quills. It was possible to slide the rod along the ground on the hazel while keeping the noose roughly horizontal.

> The St. Kildans, one and all, seemed to exercise a kind of uncanny fascination over the Puffins, which they caught one after another with the utmost ease ... So successful are the St. Kildans at this kind of sport that Angus Gillies once bagged to his own rod no less than six hundred and twenty Puffins in a single day.[29]

Kearton considered himself deft with a fly-rod, but he had enormous difficulty in catching a puffin. It was hard to stalk the bird or judge the length of the rod, let alone pull it tight at the appropriate moment, in spite of the vast numbers of Tammy Nories perched impudently on the turf.

> Some idea may be gathered of the plenitude of Puffin life at St. Kilda when it is stated, on the authority of Mr. Sands, who lived there for about nine months, that in one year alone close upon ninety thousand birds of this species were killed by the natives. They are plucked, split open like kippers, cured, and hung up to dry on strings stretched across the cottages; and whenever a native feels hungry he simply pulls one down from the line, flings it on the fire to grill, and forthwith has his lunch ...[30]

Another delicacy, though procured with more difficulty, was the 'guga' or young gannet. Under the Protection of Birds Act, 1954, the gannet was protected, but the inclusion of a clause to exempt the Nessmen and allow them to continue to take the 2,000 guga from the island of Sula Sgeir, which they have done since earliest times, shows the importance of this tradition. In 1991 John Beatty, a landscape photographer, accompanied the ten fowlers from Ness on what is a form of late-summer pilgrimage. He has provided a thoughtful and detailed account on which this description is based.[31]

Hugh Munro recorded the seabird harvest on Sula Sgeir and it seems probable that in earlier times the eider duck as well as the guga was hunted. It must have always been a dangerous business; the journey in open boats and the prospect of working on what is merely a 600m length of slippery, wave-washed rock without even a water supply. But there are three beehive-type dwellings, annually maintained and the remains of a chapel.

The best eating comes from the fledgling gannet identified by the downy tufts still clinging to head, back and legs. Younger, and more downy, they have little meat; older and sleeker they are difficult to catch. The fowlers use a long pole finished with a sprung metal jaw to lift the birds from the nests. They are killed instantly with a stout stick and their heads cut off. There are so many nests that 200 birds can be taken in half an hour. Each bird can weigh 9lbs, so the carrying them up the cliffs for plucking and gutting is a huge job. The birds are singed, de-winged, split and piled up with salt for pickling. Three birds were enough to feed twelve people.

> First, we washed the filleted birds thoroughly, winkling out all the salt. Already I could see this was going to be a greasy affair. Each bird was cut into four portions, each one scraped scrupulously clean with a small sharp knife. Cooking was simple: boiled for one hour, with a water-change after thirty minutes. It was traditional to eat guga only with boiled potates.
>
> That same evening at eight o'clock, in gathering darkness, we all arrived, especially cleaned up for the feast. The huge pot was standing on the peats with the gugas bubbling and frothing in the brown water. Potatoes were lifted from the pot and distributed amongst the twelve. Some of us had breast meat and extra skin,

> some just skin and claws and a little meat, but each portion was even in size ... we were to pull the meat apart with our fingers ... It had the texture of good steak and the taste of kipper. It had a definite sense of being from the sea. It was neither fish nor fowl, but somewhere in between.[32]

Back in Lewis, supply does not meet demand and the guga bought by the people queuing at the harbour are kept for celebrations and special occasions.

to cook guga

Method

Scrub it well with washing-soda, until it is as white as possible.
Cook in a pan of boiling water for one and a half hours.
The modern housewife boils it again in fresh water to make it less salty.

To Serve
Eat the guga with potatoes boiled in their jackets.[33]

As for the fowlers

> The whole world seemed to be present to greet us back from the ocean, to welcome their heroes with lighted lamps.[34]

These are the spiritual descendants of the men Martin observed 300 years earlier, who carried fowls home to their wives and sweethearts as marks of affection.[35] Seabirds provided strong-tasting, highly nutritious food, but fit and well-motivated men were needed to procure them. When the young bird catchers came home to report good hunting, remembered Christina McQueen,

> ... the old man would lay his hand upon the shoulder of his son, and say a blessing thrice o'er and tell him he was a man of Hirt.[36]

The lean, agile fowlers who look out from the early photographs and the athletes described by Martin were the heroes of their communities. They brought home a rich harvest. Some met tragic ends. In Fair Isle Scott heard the terrible story of

> a fine boy of fourteen (who) had dropped from the cliff ... into a roaring surf, by which he was instantly swallowed up. The unfortunate mother was labouring at the peat-moss at a little distance. These accidents do not, however, strike terror into the survivors. They regard the death of an individual engaged in these desperate exploits, as we do the fate of a brave relation who falls in battle, when the honour of his death furnishes a balm to our sorrow.[37]

When Mrs. Margaret Campbell visited the island during May 1930 she found a different situation. Sickness and the debilitating effects of tourism had taken their toll on the community.

> It was St. Kilda's Queen's Nurse, Miss Barclay, who told us that the people were close to starvation. She had been there a couple of years and she told me that five of the men there had duodenal ulcers. There was hardly one able to do hard physical work ... The islanders had become such beggars that the trawlermen wouldn`t give them anything. The deep sea trawlers would go in to shelter and if the St. Kildans went out in their small boats to ask for food, they turned the hoses on them.[38]

References — chapter 7

1. The repeal of the Salt Tax in 1817 lowered the price and improved supply
2. Kearton, R., *With Nature and a Camera*, London 1904 pp.11,12
3. Hibbert, S., *A Description of the Shetland Islands*, Lerwick, 1931, pp.315,316
4. Martin, Martin, *A Description of the Western Isles of Scotland circa 1695*, Edinburgh 1984 p.159
5. *Scottish Country Life Archive*, National Museums of Scotland.
6. Fenton, A., Traditional Elements in the Diet of the Northern Isles of Scotland. *Reports from The Second International Symposium for Ethnological Food Research*, Helsinki, August 1973
7. Cameron, Archie, *Bare Feet and Tackety Boots*, Luath Press 1988 p.61
8. *The Scottish Ethnological Archive*, National Museums of Scotland
9. Boyd, J.M., *A Habitable Land*, Edinburgh, 1966 pp.24,25
10. Martin, Martin *A Description of the Western Isles of Scotland circa 1695*, Edinburgh 1984 p.161
11. *Ibid.*, pp.427,428
12. *Ibid.*, p.408
13. *Ibid.*, p.433
14. Nicolson, J.R., *Traditional Life in Scotland*, London 1990 pp.35,36
15. Martin, *A Description of the Western Isles of Scotland circa 1695*, Edinburgh 1984 pp.429,430
16. Quine, David A., *St. Kilda Portraits* 1988 pp.74,75
17. *Ibid.*, p.21
18. Kearton, R., *With Nature and a Camera*, London 1904 p.124
19. quoted by Maclean, Charles, *Island on the Edge of the World*, New York, 1980 p.69
20. from *Annlan is Eile,* The Nicolson Institute, Stornoway, Lewis 1978
    Cormorant Brochan. Cleaned cormorant or puffin could be boiled for two hours with barley meal or oatmeal added to make a brochan or soup.
21. *The Scottish Ethnological Archive*, National Museums of Scotland
22. *The Orcadian*, 23 September 1971
23. Scott, Walter, *The Voyage of the Pharos*, Scottish Library Association 1998 p.71
24. Kearton, R., *With Nature and a Camera*, London 1904, p.119
25. Maclean, Charles, *Island on the Edge of the World*, New York 1980, p.95
26. *Scots Magazine*, May 1931, p.103
27. Kearton, R., *With Nature and a Camera*, London 1904 p.323
28. *Scots Magazine*, May 1931 pp.101,102
29. Kearton, R., *With Nature and a Camera*, London 1904 p.81
30. *Ibid.*, p.113

31. Beatty, John, *Sula, The sea-bird hunters of Lewis*, London 1992
32. *Ibid.*, p.99
33. *Annlan is Eile*, The Nicolson Institute, Stornoway, Lewis, 1978
34. Beatty, John, *Sula, The sea-bird hunters of Lewis*, London 1992 p.129
35. Martin, Martin, *A Description of the Western Isles of Scotland circa 1695*, Edinburgh 1984 p.316
36. *Scots Magazine*, May 1931, p.103
37. Scott, Walter, *The Voyage of the Pharos*, Scottish Library Association 1998 p.39
38. Shaw, M.F., *From the Alleghenies to the Hebrides*, Edinburgh 1993 p.93

'Bliss', Erskine Nicol.

Chapter 8: Conclusions
" ... famine in their aspect ..."

I could wish the public bounty, or private charity, would found in fit parts of the isles or mainland, magazines of meal, as preservatives against famine in these distant parts.

Pennant, Thomas, *A Tour in Scotland and Voyage to the Hebrides, 1772,* Edinburgh 1998 p.271

Though the sky is often sunless, the climate is mild, and the pure air of the Atlantic goes a long way to counteract the malodorous and poisonous gases ... Thus, the health of the people as a whole is satisfactory.

Report to the Secretary for Scotland on the Social Conditions of the people of Lewis in 1901, Glasgow 1902 p.cix

The doctor does not think that the poverty is of such a pressing nature as that of the poor in the town slums. A woman will never see a neighbour starve. In certain villages in the west of Lewis it was customary every time a boat came in to set aside so many fish for widows and children.

Doctor, Harris, 1914

Dr. A. C. Miller, Medical Officer of Health in Fort William was a member of the Dewar Committee, appointed by the Treasury on the eve of the First World War to investigate the medical needs of the Highlands and Islands as a whole. His own district included the Small Isles, but he understood the area in its entirety.

> As they are now, the people in general offer the appearance of well-proportioned and well-nourished men and women, and the standard is well worthy to be preserved.[1]

Almost 250 years before, Martin Martin, also a medical man, had similarly found the Lewis men to be,

> well proportioned, free from any bodily imperfections, and of a good stature ... They are a healthful and strong-bodied people, several arrive to a great age.[2]

On diet he wrote,

> they generally eat but little flesh ... Their ordinary diet is butter, cheese, milk, potatoes, colworts, brochan (porridge) and, naturally, bread.[3]

Miller also makes note of diet.

> Food - the staple food of the rural inhabitants consists of milk, oatmeal, potatoes, fish, fowl, eggs ...[4]

Although conditions varied dramatically, this rural diet, unchanged for centuries and apparently limited, was probably better than that available to the urban poor of the same period. The hens (whose eggs no longer went for rent) that foraged around the houses, for example, now shared a handful of the widely consumed imported meal. In the towns even the production of hot food posed a problem. Fuel was dear and although the gas oven dates from about 1855 it was not common before the 1890s.[5] During the second half of the nineteenth century various attempts had been made to stop the marketing of impure food, culminating in the Adulteration of Food Act, 1872 which finally made it illegal to bulk up flour with chalk or coffee with chicory. Three years later the Sale of Food and Drugs Act tightened the legal machinery of inspection. But in 1900 10% of milk and 8% of bread sold in the towns was still adulterated, two basic commodities which seemed intractable.[6] Poverty and under feeding were endemic in the cites. There was an acknowledged need for malnutrition hospitals.[7] Overall, on the eve of the First World War, 10% of children in Scotland entering school showed signs of rickets, but there was a marked difference between a prevalence of rickets in the towns and their rarity in the country areas.[8]

A study of family health in Scotland commissioned by the Carnegie United Kingdom Trustees on the eve of the First World War gives an extraordinarily detailed account of the health of the islanders. To quote the introductory letter to what is a hefty document,

> ... perhaps the most interesting sections of the Report are the Special Regional Studies. These are first-hand records of living experience. They contain much that rarely finds its way into print. They are the work of men and women trained in observation and skilled in using it ... medical officers of health, general and consulting medical practitioners, inspectors of poor, health visitors, nurses ...[9]

Conclusions:
" ... famine in their aspect ..."

In the matter of nutrition, the tentative conclusions of the report are firstly that food was, for many, at the margin of subsistence. It was probably adequate, where milk was available, but milk was not always available, particularly on the smaller crofts. Growing children were not always getting enough to eat. They were being fed irregularly and inappropriately, even where there were no shortages. There was a serious lack of vegetables and fruit.

> Nurse stated that broth is seldom made by the villagers, and that vegetables are practically never seen. The people have very few gardens, because the product is stolen by boys.[10]

Before the First World War the causes of rickets (Vitamin D deficiency) was as yet, not understood, but it was believed to be associated with stale food. In spite of this imperfect knowlege, a good milk supply was known to be important in its prevention.

> The amount of rickets among (the Lewis children) is peculiarly interesting at present. The amount of rickets among them is found to be extremely small. Good teeth, on the other hand, are said to be extremely common ... the island children are well grown, and, on the whole, plump. It is, however, certain that, at the very best, their food supply is not superfluous. Meat, one would suppose, is rare, both in the diet of the adult and of the child; fish, less rare; porridge and milk, common. Probably the milk supply is for long periods too limited; but for a great period of the year there is always some milk available.[11]

Where milk was reasonably plentiful the people were relatively (in comparison with urban dwellers) well-fed, given that the provision of a reliable milk supply in the towns was still in its infancy. However, milk was generally short in winter. Some of the worst shortages were in Harris. A doctor practising there in 1914 noted how,

> the crofts are much subdivided and there is not food sufficient to feed several cows. Therefore, there is only one cow for several families. There is a great deficiency of milk in this island, and generally in Harris ...[12]

South Uist was notoriously short of water, as well as milk.

> The chief articles of diet are tea, barley bread, potatoes; porridge is the evening meal. Butter is scarce, also fish.[13]

In North Uist the milk supply was better. Eighteen out of 23 houses visited were crofts with two or more cows. Babies were well-nurtured but,

> the school children are not so sonsy, so brosy, as at six years of age.[14]

The evidence suggests that this subsistence diet was inadequate for growing children. The Harris boys were described as 'flabby' and in South Uist a lack of resistance to tuberculosis in later life was believed to be caused by defective feeding.[15]

The boarding-out system was a reflection of the universally held view that orphans and children with no-one to care for them would flourish better in rural areas than in towns. The mere .01% of children with rickets in rural areas were known to be boarders from Glasgow, struck by the disease when very young. Dr. Mary Menzies, reporting on their conditions in 1914 makes an important distinction between

> ... children boarded with the owners of large crofts, or with crofters who have some additional means of livelihood ... where housing is poor, the croft rent relatively low and the crofter, from the depressing effect of circumstances and climate on his character has scarcely enough energy to earn a decent living for himself and his family, potatoes, and possibly salt herring, play too prominent a part in the diet.[16]

In Tiree and Iona the crofts were prosperous and the children strikingly well cared for. The overall impression, however, is that of a haphazard way of eating.

> With regard to the meals, the old-fashioned breakfast has disappeared, and the children are given usually tea and perhaps a hard biscuit before they go to school. The man does not rise

> until nearly 12 noon, and then the family has breakfast. Children coming in at midday get the remains of the cold breakfast. They have something about 4.pm, and perhaps a good meal at night - practically a two-meal per day system. The children do not really get a good meal until the evening when porridge is cooked.[17]

It was usual for the children to snatch bread and tea before school and to be given more bread for their pockets which they ate as they walked. When reporting to the Napier Commission Duncan Stewart, schoolmaster at Waternish did not think his pupils brought anything to eat to school.

> I cannot say, for I do not see them eating. I suppose they bring a piece, because they don't go home for dinner. They must have their dinner in their pockets - oatcake and a bit of cheese when they can get it, but no milk. They don't bring any flask or bottle that I have seen.[18]

In Benbecula the nurse had felt the children needed a hot drink with their midday piece and made them cocoa at her own expense.[19]

The Northern Isles were better supplied than the Hebrides. Imported oatmeal was universally used, there were plenty of potatoes and eggs and more meat than in earlier times. Even so children were not always well-nourished. "On the whole," wrote Dr Saxby, from Unst, Shetland, whose father and grandfather had both been local doctors, "the islanders are well-fed."[20] Milk was not a problem, except in Baltasound and Uyeasound where the available supply went to feed pigs and calves. Yet even in a situation of relative prosperity and plenty he did not consider that children were always appropriately fed. Young children suffered from stomach trouble which he believed to stem from what they were given to eat, described by his patients as 'just a bit o' what we hae oorsells.' He interpreted that as,

> strong tea, well boiled, hot scones, half-cooked oatcakes, salt fish and other such rubbish which even strong people can just manage to live on.[21]

In 1773 Dr. Johnson had found tea in the tacksman's house at Grissipol and reckoned it worth a comment, especially as the house was modestly equipped; the spoons being of horn.[22] Tea became increasingly available to poorer people from the mid nineteenth century and by the 1880s had become universal in the islands. In Shetland,

> even the poorest family ... will sell their clothes, their meal, to purchase it.[23]

Trade with China had been opened up in 1833 and prices dropped accordingly.[24] The authorities considered this addiction a scourge,

> ... tea drinking is largely on the increase, and the opinion is generally entertained that it contributes in no small degree to several of the ailments that affect the inhabitants. A recent writer has sarcastically remarked that 'those who survived starvation died of the teapot'.[25]

For the people tea was a universal palliative, warm comfort in a harsh land. It cost 3s per pound at the time of the Napier Commission, when Lewis crofters were spending up to £30 a year on imported goods.

> For dinner the one that can have tea will have it. There is no milk ...[26]

observed John MacIver of Breasclete. In Mid Yell they had taken to buying syrup for their children.[27] Among the authorities there was consternation about how the tea was drunk.

> The tea drunk is always stewed and much too strong[28]

noted one Hebridean nurse. References abound to indigestion or colic.

> in the middle aged people, chiefly women, caused by the fact that they drink a very strong decoction of tea, which is so strong that it is a powerful astringent.[29]

With tea came sugar. Expanding cash incomes in the thirty years after 1850[30] made some shop produce available and the sweet tooth of the islander evolved rapidly. When money or supplies were short, as in earlier times, to satisfy a sweet tooth, children had sucked sweet, edible seaweed, in Shetland known as *hinnie-waar*[31] or chewed the raw cabbage stocks.[32]

Sugar made possible the preservation of what fruit there grew and rhubarb and gooseberries found a place in the island kailyard. Recipes like this one from Islay made their appearance.

> *Smearag*, brambleberries - gather the berries when they are ripe. Pick them and put them into a basin with a handful or two of oatmeal and some sugar. Beat them with a potato beetle, or the back of a strong spoon. Serve with milk.[33]

When F.G. Rea, schoolmaster in South Uist needed assistance to lift his peats he procured

> a seven-pound jar of sweets, of which, I had learned, all the people (from the youngest to the oldest) were very fond[34]

with a view to using them as a reward. Dr. Saxby thought sweets were eaten to excess in Unst.[35] A measure of the rarity of sugar in earlier times was the Shetland practice of giving visitors to the house after a birth a lump of this delicacy with a drop of lavender essence on it as refreshment.[36]

The St. Kildans had a particular penchant for sweets, especially bull's eyes and peppermint lozenges ...

> The men often holding out their big brown palms along with the children when 'sweeties' were being distributed ... So fully does the factor recognise the pleasure these lonely folks derive from sucking sweets, that he takes a large supply with him every year. [37]

The lack of fruit and its flavours gave sweets a particular charm for islanders.

> Sloes are the only fruits of the island. An acid for punch is made of the berries of the mountain ash: and a kind of spirit is distilled from them.[38]

This was a bitter harvest. For Archie Cameron in Rum the idea of luxury was a whole barrel of apples to sit beside his chair and eat until it was empty.[39] Very occasionally he and his siblings shared an orange between them and made the segments last as long as they could. There are plenty of heart-breaking stories of fruit washed up on various shores only to be unrecognised as food. Miss Sandison of Unst's grandfather, John Peter Sandison was born in Yell.

> Father told me how the North Yell folk were fascinated when these boxes of oranges came ashore – nobody knew what to do with them. They tried boiling them, frying them and stewing them, but thought they were disgusting and threw them out.[40]

Yet it was possible to cultivate fruit in the islands, in the 1880s the minister on St. Kilda, Mr. Fiddes, had strawberries in his garden.[41] and in the same decade fruit trees were being ordered and planted along the west wall of the great castle of Armadale – pear, cherry and plum.[42]

Curly kale and cabbage were the staple Hebridean vegetables, although in the Northern Isles leeks, onions, carrots, beets, peas and beans were all common.[43] Scott was impressed to see how in Orkney, "All vegetables grow here freely in the gardens ..."[44] Pennant refers to Ligusticum scoticorum,

> Scotch parsley, or the shunis of this island (Skye) is also much valued; in medicine, the root is reckoned a good carminative, and an infusion of the leaves is thought a good purge for calves. It is besides used as a food, either as a salad, raw, or boiled as greens.[45]

The minister at Durinish fulsomely described the Glendale Cabbage

> known and sought after not only throughout all Skye but likewise in many places on the mainland, and its immense size, combined with its delicacy of flavour, entitles it to the pre-eminence which it has attained.[46]

Garden on Iona.

This cabbage's availability to his parishioners, whose

> prevalent complaints are dyspepsia, dysentery, slow fevers, and cutaneous diseases, which are almost entirely confined to the humbler classes, and arise from lowness of diet ...[47]

is not revealed. Sleat was known as the garden of Skye and Lismore had a reputation for fertility, "the lesser vegetables grow with uncommon vigour."[48] But there is truth in Fraser Darling's observation that,

> Climate and soil have not made the Gael into a natural gardener, and in many of the crofting areas the presence of sheep is not conducive to experimentation towards growing vegetables.[49]

However, the wild carrot, *curran buidhe* was not uncommon, together with wild radish and wild parsnip.[50] Nettles played some part in the diet, particularly in the spring when men and beasts were in a low condition. Below is a recipe for a nettle soup together with some poetic advice recorded by the School of Scottish Studies.

> Put an apronful of nettles in a vessel. Cover them with boiling water. When cold, strip the leaves from the stalks, and wash the leaves in cold water. Boil in a pot, covered with water, for twenty minutes. Pour out the liquid. Add a piece of butter and a handful of meal. Beat and serve hot. People ought to take seven meals of nettles every year.[51]

> If they would eat nettles in March,
> And eat muggins in May
> So many braw maidens
> Would not turn to clay![52]

(These are two foods rich in iron.)

Other wild vegetables were eaten raw, including sorrel and watercress. Bitter vetch has a branching, underground root strung with nodules which when dried has a taste like wild liquorice, acid and sweet. Chewing it was said to ward off hunger. Children liked to dig for earth - or pig nuts, the bulbous roots of an umbelliferous plant with a slender stem and small white flowers. The 'nut' has a brown skin which is easily rubbed off and a mealy flavour. Creeping cinquefoil or silverweed were known as *brisgean*. It grows on the shore line and in earlier times it was gathered from the furrows after the plough.[53]

> They were tuberous. Raw, they had a slightly nutty taste, but much harsher. When roasted, however, they had a somewhat pleasant mealy flavour.[54]

In times of shortage these roots had great value as a substitute for potatoes or bread.

> With the advent of better times, the brisgean is not now dealt with as a staple article in the food of the people, but it still holds a place among their dainties. The juveniles devour it in its raw condition, but when it is cooked, it is not often boiled in the old way, hardly ever, but rather stewed in a little water, with a little sugar added, and is eaten either hot or cold.[55]

In early times wild spinach was so important in Eriskay that

> separate spots in the island were marked off for certain families for collecting wild spinach.[56]

This soup recipe was recorded in Aberdeenshire but shows how the plant would have been used in the islands.

> Wild spinach soup - an armful of wild spinach, washed and chopped, put in a pot with a piece of braxy and cold water, boil for half an hour, add handful of oatmeal, boil 10 mins.[57]

A recipe from Islay for a wild mustard soup was thickened with barley meal.[58] Wild foods were often, though not exclusively, famine foods. Mushrooms and other fungi had their place in the diet. *Tobhtal* is a well-known dish in Lewis made from *Slabhagan* or *slokem*, a kind of seaweed gathered from the rocks.

> After it has been well washed so as to remove all sand from it, it is boiled in a litle water and thickened to the consistency of porridge, by the addition of oat or barley meal. Salt, and a little butter are added.[59]

It may have been the same seaweed that the St. Kildans, deserately short of food in the spring of 1841 cleared from the shore along with shellfish to eat with boiled sorrel in order to stave off famine.[60] Carageen and dulse are similarly edible. Carageen will set milk into quite a palatable jelly, which could also be made from the boiled-up cast antlers of deer. Butterwort will cause milk to thicken into 'yearned milk' or junket.[61]

Although conditions varied, feeding a family in the islands required relentless labour, much of which fell to women who were already weakened by pregnancy. Without transport they carried peats for the fire and seaweed for the lazy-bed. Even when meal arrived by ship at St. Kilda,

> the men conveyed the bags ... from the steamer to the rocks in their boat, whilst the women performed the far more arduous task of carrying them on their backs up the steep path to the cottages.[62]

Walter Williamson of West Burra reported to the Napier Commission that

> The poor women work a good deal harder than many of the rich men's horses.[63]

The observation made in 1894 that,

> These islanders are a fine-looking race, the men as usual superior to the women ...[64]

contains within it an unspoken hint of the harshness of their lives. The naturalist, Kearton, with a boyish compassion, noted, with exclamations,

> Poor women of St. Kilda! Their's is a hard lot. They shoulder an immense load of dock leaves which they carry up the tremendously steep hill separating the Village from the Glen, where the cows are milked, and often fetch back an equally great load of turf in addition to their buckets of milk.[65]

The 1901 Crofters' Commission Report for Lewis observed that the duties of women had not changed since the Viking era.

> She carries the seaware or other materials for manure in a creel on her back, and sometimes tills the land; she weeds and reaps, and carries the corn and hay to the barn in autumn; she likewise carries the domestic fuel on her back from the moor, and knits her stockings as she goes in the same way as her Shetland sister knits her haps or hosiery while similarly occupied. She goes with her cattle to the shieling ... In her home she attends to the domestic requirement of her family. [66]

Measured and bureaucratic, the anonymous medical author of the special study of the the Outer Hebrides noted,

> After some seventeen years' experience of administrative consideration of the near and Outer Hebrides and the island groups of Orkney and Shetland, I can only say that in many departments of life, the administrative results in the Outer Hebrides are less satisfactory than in any other part of Scotland. [67]

The burden of self-sufficiency on smaller holdings of land was always a heavy load but especially so for families where men were compelled by need to earn money away from home. The price was a slow and general decline in health for those that were left to do the work of the land. "The women assist with the croft work," notes one doctor, briskly.

> ... when a fishing season commences early heavier work falls to the women, and more miscarriages occur. During a recent spring, the fishing season being early, the women were employed harrowing, and in four townships nine miscarriages ... occurred apparently from this cause. Each miscarriage occurred in a poor house where the mother was insufficiently nourished. [68]

Creel carrying was understood to cause kyphosis - an abnormal outward curvature of the spine commonly known as hunchback.

> The tasks which Shetland men and women had to undertake within living memory were extraordinary ... I remember when a boy my mother going off early to Lerwick, a walk of seventeen miles, and walking back carrying eight pecks of meal. Fearing that my brother and I had gone to school hungry she, without resting or taking food, baked bread and walked three miles to the school - forty miles in all. [69]

All societies can look back to a notionally more golden past. In the 1870s Alexander Carmichael recorded Catherine Macphee, cottar, Aird Mhor, Iochdar, Uist bemoaning the changes she had witnessed in the countryside during her lifetime.

> There was nothing but butter and cheese and crowdie, dairy-produce and milk, and beer of heather-tops, oat-bread, barley-bread and rye-bread, porridge and milk, meat and flesh, gruel and broth ... no jam except the kind we made ourselves ... The men have taken to sloth, and they have neither kail nor carrots, nor even a garden ... [70]

The great majority of families no longer subsisted on the produce of land or sea but relied on money sent by members of their families working in the south. The adult population, it was said, kept late hours. [71]

Tuberculosis, exacerbated by poor food,overcrowding and inadequate ventilation in house and byre afflicted both humans and cattle. [72] Since the earliest recorded period, the wealth of the islanders had rested in their cattle and ironically, the health of the people in the twentieth century continued dependent on a supply of safe local milk.

> Give us, O God, of the honey-sweet foaming milk,
> The sap and milk of the fragrant farms,
> And give us, O God, along with Thy sleep,
> Rest in the shade of Thy covenant Rock. [73]

This poignant verse is from one of just three prayers of thanks and supplication for food in the entire six volume collection of hymns and incantations recorded by the folklorist, Alexander Carmichael. An endemic dearth is apparent even in the cautiously optimistic report on conditions in the parish of Uig made by the parish medical officer as islanders were heading for the battlefields of the First World War.

> The economic condition varies much, as many are in comparitive affluence; but a large section ... slide along, living from hand to mouth - but sometimes through loss of their cattle, or on account of prolonged illness, live in very straitened circumstances. [74]

References — chapter 8

1. Mackenzie, W. Leslie, _Scottish Mothers and Children_, The Carnegie United Kingdom Trust, Dunfermline 1917 (hereafter cited as _Carnegie_) p.397
2. Martin, Martin, _A Description of the Western Isles of Scotland circa 1695_, Edinburgh 1984 p.93
3. _Ibid._, p.242
4. _Carnegie_, p.400
5. Burnett, John, _Plenty and Want_, Pelican, 1966 p.185
6. Ibid., p.263
7. _Carnegie_, p.61
8. _Carnegie_, p.236
9. _Carnegie_, p.ix
10. _Carnegie_, p.448
11. _Carnegie_, p.437
12. _Carnegie_, p.452
13. _Carnegie_, p.459
14. _Carnegie_, p.454
15. _Carnegie_, p.452
16. _Carnegie_, pp.112,113
17. _Carnegie_, p.452
18. Cameron, A. D., _Go Listen to the Crofters_, Acair 1986 p.115
19. _Carnegie_, p.456
20. _Carnegie_, p.483
21. _Carnegie_, p.485
22. Johnson and Boswell, _Journey to the Western Islands of Scotland_, Oxford 1930 p.111
23. Livingstone, W.P., _Shetland and the Shetlanders_, London 1947 p.197
24. Burnett, John, _Plenty and Want_, Pelican 1966 p.26
25. _Report to the Secretary of State by the Crofters' Commission on the Social Conditions of the people of Uist_, 1903 p.cviii
26. Cameron, A. D. _Go Listen to the Crofters_, Acair 1986 p.109
27. _Ibid._, A.D. p.39
28. _Carnegie_, p.448
29. _Carnegie_, p.452
30. Hunter, James, _The Making of the Crofting Community_, Edinburgh 1976 p.111

31. Miss Joy Sandison of Unst's personal recollections.
Alaria esculenta has a sweet rib up the centre.
32. Duncan, A., ed. *Hebridean Island Memories of Scarp*, Edinburgh 1995 p.121
33. *Tocher* 27, p.181
34. Rea, F. G., *A School in South Uist*, London 1964 p.76
35. *Carnegie*, p.486
36. *Tocher* 38, p.54
37. Kearton, R., *With Nature and a Camera*, London 1904 pp.35,36
38. Pennant, Thomas, *A Tour in Scotland and Voyage to the Hebrides, 1772,* Edinburgh 1998 p.202
39. Cameron, Archie, *Bare Feet and Tackety Boots*, Luath Press 1988 p.45
40. from Miss Sandison's personal recollections
41. Kearton, R., *With Nature and a Camera*, London 1904 p.24
"He (Mr. Fiddes) also informed me that he was at that moment disproving the assertions of horticulturists that strawberries could not be grown in so high a latitude as that in which he lived ..."
42. *Lord Macdonald's Estate Papers*, Clan Donald Library, Armadale, Skye
43. Fenton, Alexander, *The Northern Isles: Orkney and Shetland,* Edinburgh 1978 p.421
44. Scott, Walter, *The Voyage of the Pharos*, Scottish Library Association 1998 p.49
45. Pennant, Thomas, *A Tour in Scotland and Voyage to the Hebrides, 1772,* Edinburgh 1998 p.312
46. *NSA*, vol.14.p.238
47. *NSA*, vol.14,p.326
48. Pennant, Thomas, *A Tour in Scotland and Voyage to the Hebrides, 1772,* Edinburgh 1998 p.359
49. Fraser Darling, Frank, *West Highland Survey*, Oxford 1956 p.298
50. *Transactions of the Gaelic Society of Inverness*, vol. XXX11, p.9
51. *Tocher* 14, p.240
52. *Ibid.*,
53. *Tocher* 25, p.52
54. *Transactions of the Gaelic Society of Inverness*, Vol. XXXII, p.11
55. *Tocher* 25, p.52
56. Goodrich Freer, A., *The Outer Isles*, London 1902 p.190
57. *Tocher* 17, pp.18,19
58. *Tocher* 30, p.408
59. *Tocher*, 27, p.181
60. Seton, G., *St Kilda*, Edinburgh 1980 pp.100,101
61. Saxby, M. R., *Shetland Traditional Lore*, Edinburgh 1932 p.166

62. Kearton, R., *With Nature and a Camera*, London 1904 p.8
63. Cameron, A.D., *Go Listen to the Crofters*, Acair 1986 p.39
64. Goodrich Freer, A., *The Outer Isles*, London 1902 p.403
65. Kearton, R., *With Nature and a Camera*, London 1904 p.19
66. *Report to the Secretary for Scotland by The Crofters Commission on the Social Condition of the People of Lewis, Glasgow 1902* p.xcviii
67. *Carnegie*, p.437
68. *Carnegie*, p.440
69. Livingstone, W. P., *Shetland and the Shetlanders*, Edinburgh 1947 pp.171,172
70. Carmichael, Alexander, *Carmina Gadelica* 6 vols. Edinburgh 1972 vol.3 p.351
71. *Carnegie*, p.447
72. *Carnegie*, p.491
73. Carmichael, Alexander, *Carmina Gadelica* 6 vols. Edinburgh 1972 vol.3 p.313
74. Carnegie, p.493

Bibliography

Anderson, J.	*Present State of the Hebrides*	1785
Baldwin, J.	*Fowling (Folk Life 12)*	Leeds 1974
Beatty, J.	*Sula, The Seabird-Hunters of Lewis*	London 1992
Bjorling, P. R.&Gissing, F. T.	*Peat: its use and manufacture*	London 1907
Black, M.	*A Taste of History*	London 1994
Boyd, J. Morton	*A Habitable Land*	Edinburgh 1966
Boyd, J. Morton	*Natural Environment of the Outer Hebrides*	Edinburgh 1979
Bray, E.	*The Discovery of the Hebrides*	London 1986
Brown, C.	*Feeding Scotland*	National Museums of Scotland 1996
Burnett, J.	*Plenty and Want*	London 1968
Burnett, R.	*Benbecula*	Benbecula 1986
Burton, W. G.	*The Potato*	London 1948
Buxton, B.	*Mingulay An Island & its People*	Edinburgh 1995
Cameron, Archie	*Bare Feet and Tackety Boots*	Luath Press 1988
Cameron, A. D.	*Go Listen to the Crofters*	Acair 1986
Campbell, J. L.	*Canna The Story of a Hebridean Island*	Canongate 1994
Campbell, J. L., ed.	*Hebridean Folksongs*, 3 vols.	Oxford 1969-81
Carmichael, Alexander	*Carmina Gadelica*	Edinburgh 1972
Cheape, Hugh	*Shielings in the Highlands and Islands of Scotland*	Folk Life no. 35 1996-97 pp.7-24
Cooper, Derek	*The Road to Mingulay*	London 1985
Cregeen, Eric R., ed.	*Argyll Estate Instructions 1771-1805*	Edinburgh 1964

Devine, T. M.	*The Great Highland Famine*	Edinburgh 1988
Duncan, A., ed.	*Hebridean Island Memories of Scarp*	Edinburgh 1995
ed. Gailey A., OhOgain D.	*Gold under the Furze*	Dublin 1966
ed. Wainwright, F. T.	*The Northern Isles*	London 1962
Eveleigh, David J.	*Old Cooking Utensils*	Shire 1997
Fea, Patrick	*Diary, 1766-1796*	Scotland 1997
Fenton, A	*Scottish Country Life*	Edinburgh 1976
Fenton, Alexander	*Traditional Elements in the Diet of the Northern Isles of Scotland*	Helsinki 1993
Fenton, Alexander	*The Northern Isles: Orkney and Shetland*	Edinburgh 1978
Fenton, Alexander	*Sowens in Scotland*	Folk Life,vol.12 1974
Findlay, William M.	*Oats*	Aberdeen 1956
Forbes, Bishop	*The Lyon in Mourning*	Edinburgh 1895 3 vols.
Fraser Darling, F.	*West Highland Survey*	Oxford 1956
Fraser Darling, F.	*Island Years*	London 1944
Fraser Darling, F.	*Crofting Agriculture*	Edinburgh 1945
Fraser Darling, F.	*Reith Lectures*	BBC 1970
Goodrich Freer, A.	*The Outer Isles*	London 1902
Grant, I. F.	*Highland Folk Ways*	London 1961
Grant, I. F., Cheape, H.	*Periods in Highland History*	London 1987
Gray, Malcolm	*The Highland Economy 1750-1850*	Edinburgh 1956
Hibbert, Samuel	*A Description of the Shetland Islands*	Lerwick 1931
Hope, A.	*A Caledonian Feast*	London 1989
Hunter, James	*The Making of the Crofting Community*	Edinburgh 1976

Johnson & Boswell	*Journey to the Western Islands of Scotland*	Oxford 1930
Johnson, Alison	*A House by the Shore*	London, 1996
Kearton, R.	*With Nature and a Camera*	London 1904
Leneman, L. ed	*Perspectives in Scottish Social History*	Aberdeen 1988
Levitt, I., Smout, C.	*The State of the Scottish Working-class*	Edinburgh 1979
Livingstone, W. P.	*Shetland and the Shetlanders*	Edinburgh 1947
Macdonald, C.	*Claire Macdonald's Scotland*	London 1990
Macdonald, Donald	*Lewis A History of the Island*	Edinburgh 1978
Macdonald, F. J.	*Crowdie and Cream*	London 1982
Mackenzie, A.	*The Highland Clearances*	Inverness 1883
Mackenzie, O.	*A Hundred Years in the Highlands*	Edinburgh1994
Mackenzie, W. C.	*History of the Outer Hebrides*	London 1903
Mackenzie, John Munro	*Diary,1851*	Stornoway 1994
Mackenzie, W. Leslie	*Scottish Mothers and Children*	Dunfermline 1917
Maclean, Charles	*Island on the Edge of the World*	New York 1980
Macleod, J. N.	*Memorials of Rev. Norman*	Edinburgh 1898
Macleod, John N.	*Memorials of the Rev. Norman Macleod*	Edinburgh 1898
MacNeil, C.	*Only the Sunny Days*	Glasgow 1988
Mais, S. P. B.	*Isles of the Island*	London 1934
Martin Martin	*A Description of the Western Isles of Scotland c.1695*	Edinburgh 1984
Mc Neill, F. Marian	*The Silver Bough*	Glasgow 1959 4 vols.
Mercer, John	*Hebridean Islands*	Glasgow 1974
Mitchell, Arthur	*The Past in the Present*	Edinburgh 1880
Munro, R. W. ed.	*Monro's Western Isles of Scotland*	Edinburgh 1961
Nicolson, A. ed.	*Gaelic Proverbs*	Edinburgh 1996

Nicolson, James R.	*Traditional Life in Shetland*	London 1990
Pennant, Thomas	*A Tour in Scotland and Voyage to the Hebrides, 1772*	Edinburgh 1998
Quine, D. A	*St. Kilda Portraits*	1988
Rea, F. G.	*A School in South Uist*	London 1964
Riddervold, A., & Ropeid, A.	*Food Conservation*	London 1988
Robson, M.	*Rona, The Distant Island*	Acair 1991
Salaman, R.	*The History and Social Influence of the Potato*	Cambridge 1985
Saxby, M. R.	*Shetland Traditional Lore*	Edinburgh 1932
Scott, Walter	*The Voyage of the Pharos*	Scottish Library Association 1998
Seton, G.	*St. Kilda*	Edinburgh 1980
Shaw, Frances J.	*The Northern and Western Islands of Scotland*	Edinburgh 1980
Shaw, Margaret Fay	*From the Alleghenies to the Hebrides*	Edinburgh 1993
Steven, M.	*The Good Scots Diet*	Aberdeen 1985
Stewart, Col. David	*Sketches of the Character, Manners and Present State of the Highlanders of Scotland*	Edinburgh 1822 2 vols.
Stout, Margaret B.	*The Shetland Cookery Book*	Lerwick 1965
The Nicolson Institute, Stornoway	*Annlan is Eile*	1978
Walker, Dr. John, ed. McKay	*Report on the Hebrides of 1764 and 1771*	Edinburgh 1980
Walker, John	*Economic History of the Hebrides*	1808
Warren, J.	A Feast of Scotland	London 1979
Wickham Jones, C.	*The Early Greens, in Highland Use*	ed Batchell Fort William 1991
Withrington, D. J. & Grant, I. R.	*The Statistical Account of Scotland*	Wakefield 1983

Bibliography cont.

The Statisical Account of Scotland, ed. Sir John Sinclair, Edinburgh 1791-99 (21 vols)

New Statistical Account of Scotland, Edinburgh 1845 (15 vols) [cited as *NSA*]

Report to the Secretary for Scotland by the Crofters Commission on the Social Conditions of the People of Lewis in 1901 as compared with twenty years ago, Glasgow 1902

Report to the Secretary for Scotland by the Crofters Commission on the Social Conditions of the people of Uist in 1903 as compared with twenty years ago Glasgow 1905

Scottish Mothers and Children, The Carnegie United Kingdom Trust, Dunfermline 1917

Review of Scottish Culture (*ROSC*)

Tocher, the School of Scottish Studies, Edinburgh

The Scots Magazine

Transactions of the Gaelic Society of Inverness

The Scottish Ethnological Archive, National Museums of Scotland

Lord Macdonald's Estate Papers, Clan Donald Library, Armadale, Skye

The Orcadian

Index

A

Adomnan 15, 26
Adulteration of Food Act, 1872 112
antlers 8, 39, 122
apples 118
auk 102

B

baking 15, 17, 18, 24, 25, 62, 77
Baltasound 115
bannock 14-18, 24, 25, 37, 77
Barvas ware 39
baskets 38
batter 17, 18
beastings 58
beef 58, 82-85, 92, 102
Beltane bannocks 17
bere 8, 15-19, 24, 36, 45-47
beremeal 77 (bere-meal 17, 18)
Berneray 16, 51, 98
black puddings 89
blight 48
blood 77, 84, 89, 90, 100
blubber 91
Boswell and Johnson 10, 80
brains 25, 89
brambles 8, 18
brander 17, 24
braxy 86, 87, 121
bread 13, 14, 17-19, 22-25, 29, 33, 58, 60, 61, 69, 72, 85, 111-115, 121, 124
brine 73, 76, 84, 90
British Fisheries Society 34, 74
brochan 14, 108, 111
brose 21
burstin 77
Bute 8
butter 23, 29, 46, 56, 58, 60-64, 73, 78, 102, 111, 114, 120, 122, 124
buttermilk 24, 27, 46, 62, 63
butterwort 122

C

cabbage 89, 117-119
Cameron, Archie 43, 51, 60, 66, 72, 78, 80, 81, 93, 94, 108, 118, 127, 129
Canna 8, 16, 69, 82, 98
carageen 122
Carmichael, Alexander 95, 124, 128, 129
Carron Company 37, 43
Central Board of Management for Highland Relief 19
cheese 38, 56, 58, 60-65, 75, 111, 115, 124
cherry 118
chimney 32, 33 (chimneys 33)
clapshot 46
cleits 73, 84, 96, 102
coalfish 70, 72, 77

cockles 50
cocoa 115
cod 74-78
collops 58, 89
Colonsay 19, 98
cooking pot 33, 36-39, 89
Copinsay 97
cormorant 102, 108
corn 123
cows 7, 17, 39, 51, 56, 57, 60, 61, 84, 98, 114, 123
craggans 40, 41, 59
cream 15, 23, 38, 58, 59, 62-64, 77, 78, 131
crofts 74, 75, 113-115
crowdie 63, 124, 131
curds 62, 63
Curl 48
currants 89

D

Da Pukkle 23, 27
Dewar Committee and Report on the Condition of Medical Service in the Highlands and Islands 1912 111
dogfish 70, 74
dulse 122
Duncan, Angus 18, 24, 59, 63, 90
dung 30

E

Eday 31
eggs 18, 29, 75, 96-100, 103, 112, 115
eider duck 97, 105
Eigg 8
Eriskay 7, 30, 31, 53, 71, 121

F

Fair Isle 19, 88, 106
famine 8, 14, 17-21, 26, 47, 49-54, 70, 71, 91, 110, 122, 129
fat 46, 84, 89-91, 96, 100, 102
feathers 96, 101
fire-tongs 36
fireplaces 28, 34
fish roe
flounders 71, 72
flour 17, 23, 24, 50, 78, 89, 112
Foula 60, 96, 97, 100
fowling 96-101, 104, 129
Fraser Darling, Frank 31, 42, 44, 54, 55, 58, 66, 120, 127, 130
fuel 30, 31, 42, 47, 112, 123
fulmar 61, 96, 98-103

G

gannet 8, 95, 98-101, 104, 105
Gingich 98
Glendale cabbage 119
goats 56, 58, 86, 87
graddan 22
grain 14-16, 19, 22, 23, 27, 45, 47, 49, 57, 61, 85, 88
Grant, I. F 38, 42,,43, 67, 80, 93, 130, 132?.
guga 96, 99, 105, 106, 109

guillemots 96, 97
gurnards 72

H
haddock 72, 77
haggis 90
ham 58, 75, 103
Harris 15, 16, 48, 51, 57, 59, 102, 103, 111, 113, 114
heart 50, 89, 90, 118
hearths 30, 33
heather 34, 38, 51, 52, 69, 124
Heisgeir 91
herring 7, 47, 76, 78, 81, 90, 114
Heskir 30
Highland Folk Museum, Kingussie 30, 33, 37, 41, 43, 93
Highland Quarter Cakes 17
hinnie-waar 117
hogs 88
honey 18, 125
horses 31, 50, 122
Hoy 88
hungmill 59
husks 23

I
Iona 15, 69, 115

J
Jura 19, 29, 32, 38, 64, 71

K
kale 118
Kearton, Richard 10, 39, 43, 66, 70, 80, 93, 94, 101-104, 108, 123, 127, 128, 131
kelp 19, 37, 46, 47, 52, 74
kettles 28, 37, 41
kipper 104, 106
kittywakes 96, 98, 102
kloks 62
knockin stane 35
kyphosis 124

L
lapwing 98
lazy-bed 8, 45, 48, 122
Lewis 20, 21, 24-29, 39, 40, 43, 50, 53, 54, 59-62, 66-69, 75, 77, 80-83, 86-89, 93-96, 106-113, 116, 122, 123, 128-131, 133
limpets 29, 71, 72, 91
ling 74-78
liver 24, 71, 76-78, 89, 90
liver krolls 24, 77
lungs, *lights* 32, 89
lyres 96

M
Macdonald, Donald 26, 43, 54, 63, 67, 80, 81, 93, 94, 131
Macdonald, Father Allan 21
Mackenzie, Osgood 51, 54
MacLachan, Alice 83, 101

Macleod, Dr Norman, *Caraid nan Gaidheal* *49, 54, 86, 131*
Macleod, Sir Norman 16
Macphee, Catherine 124
malnutrition 112
mart 86
Martin, Martin 10, 14, 16, 22, 43, 57, 90, 111, 131
Matheson, James 20
McQueen, Christina 106
meat 25, 37, 75, 82-87, 90-96, 101, 102, 105, 106, 113, 115, 124
milk 14-18, 21-23, 29, 38-43, 46, 47, 51-64, 69, 111-117, 122-125
Mingulay 8, 26, 97, 98, 129
Mitchell, Arthur 14, 35, 40, 42, 43, 59, 66, 131
Muck 8, 30, 94
Mull 17, 18, 60, 74, 97
mushrooms 122
mutton 7, 83, 86, 87

N

Ness 76, 96, 105
nettles 59, 120
North Rona 31, 98
North Ronaldsay 31

O

oatcakes 24, 25, 60, 61, 64, 115, 116
oats 13-15, 18, 19, 23, 26, 27, 35, 45, 47, 48, 130
offal 88, 90, 102
oil 18, 41, 61, 71, 78, 91, 96, 101, 102
onions 102, 118
oon 58
oranges 59, 118
Orkney 8, 10, 14-19, 23, 30, 31, 35, 45, 60, 62, 76, 89, 91-97, 102, 118, 123, 127, 130
ovens 24, 25, 33, 37, 41, 62, 77, 112

P

pancake 14, 37
parsley 119
pears 118
pease flour 17
peat 7, 10, 24, 29-37, 40-42, 46, 51, 103-106, 117, 122, 129
Pennant, Thomas 10, 14-18, 26-29, 32, 38, 42-45, 57, 66-71, 80, 88, 93, 110, 118, 127, 131
Pharos 26, 30, 42, 54, 80, 81, 91, 93, 94, 108, 109, 127, 132
pigs 88, 89, 94, 115
plum 118
poaching 87
pork 75, 89, 90, 94, 101, 102
porridge 14, 17, 21-24, 29, 33, 37, 38, 46, 88, 111-115, 122, 124
potatoes 18, 29, 36, 38, 44, 45, 46, 53, 78, 105, 109, 111-115, 121
poultry, hens 7, 88, 112
prawns 8

Prince Charles Edward Stewart 24, 25, 30, 36, 61, 62, 65, 71, 73
protein 18, 44, 47, 96
puddings 89, 90
puffin 8, 98, 104, 108

Q

quaich 38
quern 7, 18, 22, 35, 36

R

rabbit 76
raisins 89
Rea, Frederick 21, 27, 42, 69, 80, 83, 117, 127, 132
Reid, John 100
remikel 38
rent 19, 20, 36, 47, 50-53, 60, 74, 83, 112, 114
rickets 112-114
ropes 29, 37, 63, 87, 95, 97-101, 103
Ross, John 101
Rum 19, 25, 29, 39, 60, 72, 85-89, 97, 118
rye 18, 57, 124

S

saithe 72, 74, 76, 78, 87
Sale of Food and Drugs Act 1875 112
salmon 34, 67, 69
salt 21, 46, 52, 62-64, 73-78, 83-90, 96, 97, 105, 108, 109, 114, 116, 122
salting 62, 74, 76, 83, 85
sausage 89, 90
Saxby, M. R. 27, 80, 81, 93, 115, 117, 127, 132
Scarp 18, 22-27, 42, 59, 63, 66, 81, 90, 94, 127, 130
scones 14, 15, 17, 23-27, 42, 59, 63, 66, 81, 90, 94, 127, 130
Scotch parsley 119
Scott, Walter 10, 26, 30, 42, 54, 80, 81, 88, 93, 94, 102, 106, 108, 109, 118, 127, 132
seabirds 83, 96-98, 101, 102, 105, 106, 129
seal 29, 91
seaweed 10, 30, 46, 48, 57, 64, 84, 117, 122
shag 8, 97, 102
Shaw, Margaret Fay 26, 109, 132
shearwater 98
sheep 7, 8, 18, 36, 39, 46, 50, 52, 56, 58, 59, 83-90, 120
shellfish 7, 71, 122
Shetland 8, 14, 19, 23, 24, 27, 31, 32, 35-39, 42-45, 56, 59-62, 66, 67, 72-81, 84-86, 91-96, 108, 115-117, 123-128, 130-132
shielings 38, 60, 62, 63, 67, 123, 129
sieves 23, 39, 63
sillock 24, 72, 77
silverweed 8, 121
skate 72, 74, 76
skeo, skeos 73, 96
skins 36, 46
Skye 8, 14, 16, 18, 22, 32, 41, 57, 70, 85, 88, 92, 94, 119, 120, 125, 127, 133
skyle 32

slabhagan 122
slabhraidh 32
sloes 118
smearag 117
smoke 28-32, 83
sorrel 121, 122
soup 14, 21, 33, 34, 85, 89, 102, 108, 120, 121, 122
South Uist 7, 9, 21, 27, 33, 42, 45, 69, 71, 80, 83, 114, 117, 127, 132
sowens 23, 24, 27, 130
span 38, 98
sparls 89, 90
speun mate 14
spinach 121
St. Kilda 8, 36, 38, 56, 61, 67, 70, 71, 87, 96-104, 107, 108, 117, 118, 122, 123, 132
St. Columba 7, 15, 26
starch 44, 47
Stornoway 34, 45, 61, 76, 80, 93, 108, 109, 129, 131
straw 18, 22, 39, 64
strawberries 118, 127
Struan Mìcheil 17
sugar 33, 47, 60, 84, 85, 89, 117, 121
Sula Sgeir 96, 98, 105
swats 23
swee 33
sweets 117, 118
Swona 71

T

tea 32, 33, 100, 114-117
tinkers 39
Tiree 16, 30, 75, 115
tobhtal 122
trout 69
tuberculosis 114
turf 15, 28, 30, 47, 50, 99, 104, 123
turnips 46, 48, 57, 85
tusk 74

U

Unst 9, 75, 91, 115, 117, 118
Uyeasound 115

V

vegetables 7, 31, 46, 47, 85, 113, 118-121
venison 8, 85

W

wages 19, 45
Walker, Dr. John 10, 54, 57, 61, 66, 72, 80, 83, 91, 132
watercress 121
whale 90, 91, 94
whey 58, 59, 63, 65
whiting 74
wild carrot 120
wild mustard 122
wild parsnip 122
wild radish 120
winkles 7, 71